North Carolina Wesleyan College Library

Scurry - Drum Collection
Given by:
Dr. Frank Scurry and
Carolina Evangelical
Divinity School

Take Hold of the Treasure

Take Hold of the Treasure

Life in the Christian Faith

Leonard Griffith

Judson Press® Valley Forge

TAKE HOLD OF THE TREASURE

Copyright © 1980
The Anglican Book Centre
600 Jarvis Street
Toronto, Ontario
Canada M4Y 2J6

Judson Press Edition 1983
Judson Press, Valley Forge, PA 19481

All rights reserved. No part of this publication may be reproduced, stored in a retrieval system, or transmitted in any form or by any means, electronic, mechanical, photocopying, recording, or otherwise, without the prior permission of the copyright owner, except for brief quotations included in a review of the book.

Unless otherwise indicated, Bible quotations in this volume are from the Revised Standard Version of the Bible copyrighted 1946, 1952 © 1971, 1973 by the Division of Christian Education of the National Council of the Churches of Christ in the U.S.A., and used by permission.

Other versions of the Bible quoted in this book are:
The New English Bible, Copyright © The Delegates of the Oxford University Press and The Syndics of the Cambridge University Press, 1961, 1970.

The Holy Bible, King James Version.

Library of Congress Cataloging in Publication Data

Griffith, Leonard, 1920-
  Take hold of the treasure.

  Includes bibliographical references.
  1. Theology, doctrinal—Popular works. I. Title.
BT77.G86 1983   230   82-23250
ISBN 0-8170-0997-3

The name JUDSON PRESS is registered as a trademark in the U.S. Patent Office.
Printed in the U.S.A.

*for Jane
and
her parents*

CONTENTS

Introduction 9

Why Not the Best? 11
Why not a personal God? 13
Why not Jesus Christ? 20
Why not Christian Commitment? 27
Why not the Church? 35
Why not the Resurrection? 42

The Best is the Greatest 49
An Example of Great Faith 51
Christ is Greater than Religion 58
The First Great Duty of Religion 66
A Great Price for a Greater Treasure 74
What is True Greatness? 82

The Greatest is Forever 89
Words that Never Pass Away 91
The Love that Never Separates 98
The Friend who Never Fails 105
A Rule that Never Changes 112
Life that Never Ends 120

Notes 127

INTRODUCTION

This is a book about evangelism — not its methods and techniques but its essential message, the unchanging and everlasting gospel of Jesus Christ. I can say with Paul, "Of this gospel I was made a minister . . ." (Eph. 3:7 RSV). I can say also that, after proclaiming it in many places for more than thirty years, I am convinced more than ever that it is the power of God for salvation.

Though the gospel remains constant, the world continually changes in its response. Canadians responded eagerly during the post-war years when I began my ministry. They flocked into the churches, hungering for a Word of God that would comfort them for past catastrophes and give them hope for the future. Those were heady and exciting years for preachers. We thought they would last forever. But the picture changed overnight, and people began staying away from church for a variety of reasons. Some questioned the Christian faith itself. Others held on to the faith but let go their grip on institutional religion. Some decided that the church was out of touch with the real issues of life. Others with more affluence and leisure time simply adopted new life styles that left no room for weekend church attendance.

Meanwhile, my incurably optimistic friends kept telling me that the tide would turn and the empty pews would begin to fill up again. I wanted to believe them but couldn't, partly because I spent six years preaching in Britain where I saw how low the church can sink in popular esteem. Now, I admit that I was wrong. We may have lost the greater part of a generation. But a new generation has grown up — young people who want to explore the faith which their parents rejected and the institution which their parents ceased to support. A few parents are coming back too.

The most encouraging sign in my recent experience has been a series of three annual Parish Missions in St. Paul's Church, Bloor Street, Toronto, where I serve on the clergy staff. They were initiated by some of the lay people who got busy on the telephone and persuaded many of our members to bring their friends to Sunday worship. That sounds a simple thing to do, except that they were to invite friends who had not been inside a church for years. They rose to the occasion, and the results exceeded our highest expectations. Indeed, we were so encouraged by the first two missions, held each year in the post-Easter period, that we planned the third for July, the hottest month of the summer, when our city is almost deserted on weekends. Even then the response was heartening.

Those were low-key missions during which I preached sermons dealing with the basic issues of the Christian faith and calling for Christian commitment. I took it for granted that many people who stand outside the church are not antagonistic to the church or to the gospel — in fact, their lives are often fine advertisements for the faith which they don't profess. They already have what is good. I challenged them to accept the best, God's best, Jesus Christ. I proclaimed to them that the Best is the Greatest and the Greatest is Forever. I reminded them that, in a time of transience when everything seems disposable, the church still offers them that which is lasting and permanent.

In all my years of preaching I have never presented sermons that evoked such an enquiring and appreciative response. Certainly they quickened the life of our own congregation, they kindled fires in hearts which had gone cold, they confirmed my own faith in the power of the historic gospel. They appear in the following pages with the prayer that through them the Spirit of God will continue to speak.

L.G.

Why Not the Best?

WHY NOT A PERSONAL GOD?

A boy and a girl came to my office to arrange for their wedding. Without embarrassment they told me that they had been living together for the better part of a year, and they guessed how I felt about that. But I tried to be positive and assure them that they would find in Christian marriage a happiness that could come to them in no other way. I told them that marriage is one of God's best gifts to his children; and if they loved each other enough to want what is good for each other, why not the best?

Then we proceeded to make plans for the ceremony. They had some definite ideas about the kind of ceremony they wanted. They said that the officiating minister must not address God as if he were a person, because that would be offensive to some of the guests; he must speak to God and refer to God using such impersonal terms as *truth* and *power*, *love* and *life*. I admired their honesty and told them so, but I reminded them gently that since they had chosen to be married in a church, they ought to be prepared to accept the church's ceremony. Then I said to the young man, "Evidently God rates lower with you than the girl you are going to marry." When he looked puzzled, I continued, "This lovely girl is a person, and personality is the highest we know, far higher than abstract principles like truth and power, love and life. Are you willing to say that God is less than the highest we know?"

I was asking him, "Why not the best?" That's a question to be asked of all sorts of people, not just atheists. There are very few real atheists in our society. Most people, whether or not they attend church or profess to be religious, believe in some kind of God. Their god may be an abstract principle like love, truth, justice; a life force, first cause, intelligent designer; or the ground and depth of our being. Their religious faith is expressed in a poem, popular a few years ago, entitled "Each in his own Tongue," where the verses describe the development of life, the beauty of nature, the yearnings of the heart, and the devotion to duty and conclude by saying, "Some call it Evolution, or Autumn, or Longing, or Consecration ... and others call it God."[1]

The best we know about God is not evolution, autumn, longing, or consecration; it is the image that Jesus gave when he taught us to address God as Father. That is an intensely personal idea of God. A father is a person just as you are a person. He thinks and feels, listens and answers, loves and hates, acts and reacts. That's how Jesus thought of God, that's how he spoke of God, and that's how he always addressed God in his prayers. When the disciples asked him to teach them how to pray, he said, "Begin your prayer by saying, 'Our Father'." Actually a better translation would be "Daddy" — a very intimate form of address that has the overtones of affection, trust, and dependence which parents cherish because it makes them feel like parents. You were never as big a man in the eyes of your children, never so important to them, and never so needed by them as when they called you "Daddy." Jesus gave us that image of God when he said, "If you, then, bad as you are, know how to give your children what is good for them, how much more will your heavenly Father give good things to those who ask him." (Matt. 7:11 NEB). That is the best we know about God. Think what it means.

I   It means that he is a God *we have to deal with*. There is an old legend about the devil briefing his minions. To the first he says, "What will you tell people?" The answer comes back. "I'll tell them that there is no God." "That's no good," says the devil. "They won't believe you." He turns to the second and asks, "What will you tell them?" "I'll tell them that there is a God but that he doesn't love them." "No good. They won't believe that either." He turns to the third minion. "What will you tell men?" "I'll tell them that there is a God who loves them but that it doesn't matter." "Fine," says the devil, "off you go."

That's the whole point. God as an impersonal life-force or an abstract principle at the heart of things doesn't matter. He is a nobody, he could be replaced by a computer, he is not a God with whom we have to do. That serves the purpose of evil very well. We can leave that God out of our calculations; we can disobey him, because there is no one to disobey. The world becomes like a classroom without a teacher or like a city where the police have gone on strike. The citizens can meet and make a few ad hoc rules, but who administers and enforces them? As Dostoevski said, "Cease to believe in God, and everything is permitted."

But what a different picture if we believe that God is a Father and that he is related to us as a human father is related to his children!

Then everything is not permitted, because we are responsible to such a God. He is a God with whom we have to do. We may disobey him as children growing up in their father's house may disobey their father. We may even turn our backs on him as the Prodigal Son did when he left home and emigrated to a far country. Even when far away, he still had to reckon with his father. Everything that happened to him reminded him (at least negatively) of his father: "How many hired servants of my father's have bread enough and to spare, and I perish with hunger?" At last he said, "I will arise and go to my father." So he went home, and his father welcomed and forgave him even before he had time to say that he was sorry (Luke 15:11vv).

That old story should really be called The Parable of the Loving Father. Jesus intended it to be a picture of God. He wanted us to know that God's love for his children is active, persistent, dynamic, that it follows us wherever we go. We can never get away from it. Many people have discovered that truth in their own experience. One of them was the poet Francis Thompson, who started his life as a medical student and became addicted to drugs and lost himself in poverty in the slums of London. From that wretched condition he was rescued for the enrichment of English literature and the world by friends in whom he recognized the love of God. He came to realize that even though he had made his bed in the hell of misery and the darkness of despair, even though he had secluded himself from men and fled to the uttermost bounds of loneliness, he could not escape the pursuing love of God. Out of a full heart he wrote:

> I fled Him, down the nights and down the days;
>   I fled Him, down the arches of the years;
> I fled Him, down the labyrinthine ways
>   Of my own mind; and in the mist of tears
> I hid from Him, and under running laughter.
>   Up vistaed hopes, I sped;
>   And shot, precipitated,
> Adown Titanic glooms of chasmèd fears,
> From those strong Feet that followed, followed after.
>   But with unhurrying chase,
>   And unperturbèd pace,
> Deliberate speed, majestic instancy,

> They beat — and a Voice beat
> More instant than the Feet —
> 'All things betray thee, who betrayest Me.'²

That is the best that we can believe about God. Why not the best?

II The father God is not only a God we have to deal with; *he is a God who is on our side.* The opening sermon at the 1954 General Assembly of the World Council of Churches was preached by Bishop Bromley Oxnam of the Methodist Church in the United States. He spoke proudly and gratefully of his father, the old-fashioned type who wanted what was good for his children and who did not hesitate to bring them into line. The bishop said that he chafed under the discipline at times, but added, "I always knew one thing about my father — he was *for* me. Whatever he did was for my good; he was on my side." The supreme truth about the God whom Jesus pictured as our heavenly Father is that he wants what is good for us; he is indeed on our side. Some people have never heard the truth or, if they have heard it, don't really believe it. They think that God is as neutral, indifferent, and impersonal as an IBM computer. From their struggles, suffering, and moral failure they cry out cynically in the words of the psalmist, "How can God know? Is there knowledge in the most High?" (Ps. 73:11 RSV).

Others think that God is against them, and they are right. God may be against us, not as a policeman against breakers of the law, but as a loving Father against the child who betrays his love. Surely God is against political regimes that torture people, deprive them of freedom, and allow them to starve; against industries that pollute the sky, and mining enterprises that rape the earth; against unemployment and racial discrimination, and movies that exploit sex. That's what the Bible means by the wrath of God — which is a terrible thing, although not the worst thing that could happen to us. A worse fate than the wrath of God would be the indifference of God, rejection by God. The wrath of God is still grace. That God is against us shows that he still cares for us, still loves us, still wants the best for us. God may be so much against us that he is *for* us.

How does God prove to us that he is on our side? There is a story about a farmer who asked that question and gained a new insight into the meaning of the incarnation. One day in the late autumn, after a spell of mild weather, a sudden storm came up, a blinding blizzard that shook the trees and buildings. Stepping outside, he noticed the birds shivering on the ground. They couldn't fly against the driving wind, and it seemed that they would freeze to death. The farmer wondered what he could do for those poor creatures. If only he could get them to take refuge in the barn! He flung open the barn door and switched on the lights, then went outside and tried to drive the birds in, but he only drove them further away. They saw him as an enemy and no less a threat than the storm. How could he convince them that he was their friend? He realized that he would have to become a bird himself and fly into the barn ahead of them. That led him to realize that God must become a man and walk the road of life ahead of us to show us that he is not our enemy but our friend.

That's what God has done. In Jesus Christ, who was bone of our bone and flesh of our flesh, God has come where we are, thrown in his lot with us, made our life his life, our peril his peril, our suffering his suffering. One of the most precious names that the Bible gives to Jesus is "Emmanuel, God with us" (Matt. 1:23) — which could mean "God beside us and God for us." Paul spells it out when he asks rhetorically, "If God be for us, who can be against us?" (Rom. 8:31 KJV). That's the kind of question we ask of a personal God. We ask it when illness and pain torture our bodies and spirits, and we can't take any more. We ask it when we do our best to stand for truth and right, and men mock our ideals. We ask it when the forces of evil assault our souls, and we wonder how much longer we can resist. We ask it when men lose hope, because the world's great problems seem beyond our wisdom and ability to solve. "If God be for us, who can be against us?" A God for us, a God on our side. That is the best we can believe about God.

III The Father God is not only a God with whom we have to do, a God on our side; *he is a God to whom we can pray.* The former Bishop of Woolwich says in one of his books, "I am sure that large numbers both of clergy and laity have simply given up praying."[3] That's not surprising. People cease to pray because they have ceased to believe, or perhaps never did believe, in a personal God. You can't pray to an abstract principle at the heart of the universe. You can't pray to the ground and depth of your being.

Prayer is like talking into a telephone. You have to know that there is a listener at the other end of the line, a person who hears and answers you one way or another, or you feel like a fool. The God to whom we can pray must be a God who not only listens to us but loves us. The words of Jesus have to be true: "If you, then, bad as you are, know how to give your children what is good for them, how much more will your heavenly Father give good things to those who ask him" (Matt. 7:11).

It was on the basis of those words that Jesus taught his disciples to pray. That was the only thing the disciples ever asked Jesus to teach them. They were praying men themselves but they never realized that prayer could be as real as it was with Jesus. When he knelt, they could see that something was happening, and when he rose from his knees, they knew something had happened. "Teach us to pray like that," they cried eagerly. Jesus replied, in effect, "How you pray depends on what you believe about God. If you believe that he is a person and that he loves you as a father loves his children, you can present to him the whole range of human need — great things like the coming of his kingdom and small things like the provision of daily bread." "Our Father, who art in heaven. Hallowed be thy name..." (Luke 11:1vv).

Some may say, "If God is a loving Father, why must we pray to him at all? Surely he already knows the things that we need and will do what is best for us whether or not we ask him. He has a father's plans for his children. Can our prayers prevail upon God to change his plans and deal with us differently than he otherwise might?" One preacher considered that question in an unusual sermon entitled, "Does God Read His Children's Mail?" He asked, "What if God is too much of a gentleman for that sort of thing? What if he is too honourable a Father ever to steam open some sealed flap of our thinking, ever to take some thin envelope of our minds and hold it up against the light of his eternal vigilance? What if God, even though he could, refuses to read our letters unless they bear his name and address?"[4]

So we send our letters to God, plainly marked with his name and address. Why doesn't he answer them? The truth is that God does answer them, but not always in the way we expect or want. Loving parents don't give their children everything they ask for. They don't say Yes every time. However much they hate to do it, they sometimes say No or Wait, because they love their children and want what is good for them. Sometimes God says No or Wait because he loves us and because he knows what is good for us better than we know ourselves. We must never think that God does not answer our prayers. God answers every prayer. He is our Father who loves us infinitely more than we love our children, and we can expect from him infinitely more than our children can expect from us.

The spine-chilling book, *Alive!*[5] by Piers Paul Read is the true story of a plane crash high in the Andes Mountains where sixteen of the forty-five passengers and crew survived. It is a story of disaster and tragedy, of heroism and sacrifice, of mutual aid and tender care for the injured, sick, and dying. It is also a story of faith and prayer, of stalwart young men linking hands each night, saying their rosary together, pleading with God to save them, and then in the end giving thanks to God for their rescue. The survivors felt very certain that God had answered their prayers. They considered that to have survived the plane crash, to have escaped being killed by a terrible avalanche, and to have stayed alive for ten weeks in spite of excruciating cold and gnawing hunger, could be ascribed only to the hand of God. They felt sure that God had played a fundamental role in their survival, that he had been there, present on the mountain. Indeed they felt that they had been closer to God than they had ever been or ever would be, and that as a result of what had happened, their lives could not possibly be the same again.

That's what it means to believe in a personal God, a God with whom we have to do, who is on our side, and to whom we can pray. That is the image of God that Jesus gave when he taught us to address God as Father. It is the best we know about God. So why not the best?

... NOT JESUS CHRIST?

The 1960s and early '70s were hurricane years for the Christian religion — years when the rough winds of cynicism and secularism swept away many of the old certainties and left the landscape littered with the wreckage of faith. Only Jesus came out of the storm unscathed. He emerged stronger than ever. Even when they stopped praying and ceased to believe in God and turned their backs on the church, many people still said they admired Jesus. They still clung to him, if only as a folk-hero with whom they could identify in his idealism and his life lived for others. The humanists of our time have said some beautiful things about Jesus, the Man of Galilee, and we can only be grateful to them. Yet to the humanists of our time and to many others we say this: "If you can believe such good things about Jesus, why not read the New Testament and try to believe the best? Why not get to know all sides of his personality, so that he can be to you all that he is to us who know him as the Christ, the Son of the living God?"

In my childhood I knew the child Jesus. I pictured him as a baby in Bethlehem nestled in Mary's arms and then as a toddler in the Nazareth home running to his mother for comfort. How wonderful that Jesus came into the world as a gurgling infant! We can teach our children to know and love him and to lisp his precious name as soon as they begin to talk.

In my boyhood Jesus became for me the pattern of ideal growth. That was because I belonged to a boys' club at the church which took as its motto the words from Luke's Gospel: "And Jesus increased in wisdom and stature, and in favour with God and man" (2:52 KJV). We were taught to think of the boy Jesus growing up in Nazareth and developing, as we ought to develop, in four different facets of personality: mentally "in wisdom," physically "in stature," spiritually "in favour with God," and socially "in favour with man."

In my youth I became attracted to the human Jesus. I thought of him as a strong, muscular, red-blooded man. A book that caught my imagination in those days was Bruce Barton's *The Man Nobody Knows*. I liked his description of Jesus, with a scourge of cords in his hand, striding into the temple and knocking the tables of the moneychangers in all directions. When I read of how this magnetic leader walked along the seashore and called men from their fishing boats, I thought, "If Jesus walked by today and called me, I should leave everything, as the disciples did, and follow him."

Later I came to admire Jesus the teacher. I studied his parables and the Sermon on the Mount and thought to myself, "Here is the highest wisdom ever given to the human race. Here is the answer to the world's problems. If men would only heed those teachings and try to put them into practice, there would be no more wars or poverty or injustice, because we should live together as brothers." I was a youthful idealist in those days. I can honestly say that if I had any worthy motive for entering the ministry, it was to preach the Christian ethic, to teach people to live as the man Jesus taught us to live.

What impressed me most was that the man Jesus backed up everything that he said. He lived his ideals and in the end died for them. I saw him on Calvary's cross as the great martyr who with his dying breath could ask God to forgive those who put him there, and I worshipped him for it. Jesus of Nazareth was my hero, the one perfect man ever to emerge from an imperfect humanity, my teacher, my pattern and the leader whom I wanted to follow to the end of my days. I knew Jesus as the magnificent Man of Galilee, and that is how a great many people know him. But that is not the best.

II That knowledge by itself could never have produced the gospels or transformed human lives or made Christianity the world religion that it is today. Christianity begins by saying that there was something special about Jesus. Though he emerged from the human race, he came from beyond the human race. He brought eternity into time, he linked heaven and earth, he reconciled the natural and the supernatural, he revealed God.

That was the next stage in my understanding of Jesus, and I reached it in theological college. I have always been grateful that my teachers never used the misleading phrase "the divinity of Jesus," because that phrase does not occur in the New Testament. I have never believed that Jesus was God walking about the earth in human form. I believe that Jesus revealed God, showed us what God is like. He is a window through whom we can see into the mystery of God's nature. All that we know about God with any certainty we learn by looking at Jesus.

Even the disciples came gradually to that knowledge. At first they knew their master as the best man who ever lived, the wisest teacher who ever taught, the strongest leader who ever commanded men's loyalty, and they tried to explain him in terms of those human categories. As time went on, however, they became aware of certain facts about Jesus that those categories could not contain. There was the fact of his own immense claims, such as no one has made before or since. He called God his Father and himself God's Son — not in the general way that all men are sons of God, but in a very unique, specific, and intimate way. He said, "I and the Father are one.... He who has seen me has seen the Father" (John 10:30; 14:9 RSV).

There was also the fact that everything about Jesus supported his claims. He not only talked about God, as the prophets had done before him; he did for men everything which the prophets had foretold that only God could do. He healed the incurably sick in body and mind, he brought the dead back to life, he forgave men their sins. For centuries the Jewish people had waited and prayed for the Messiah, the Christ, God's representative who would do those very things. When Jesus, on the road to Caeserea Philippi, asked his disciples the question which they had been asking themselves, "Who do you say that I am?" the only answer they could give was the one that Peter blurted out, "You are the Christ, the Son of the living God" (Matt. 16:6 RSV).

This is a thrilling stage to reach in our Christian adventure — to look at Jesus in the gospels and say with certainty, "God is like that!" It means that in Jesus we have the absolute truth about life and the universe, the final truth to which all other truths in science, philosophy, and religion must be related. It means that we can trust all that Jesus said — his teachings about God, man, sin, and the kingdom, his promise of salvation in this world and in the world to come. It means we can believe that the way of life set before us in the Sermon on the Mount, the way of love, lowliness, and sacrifice, is the right way, the only way to human fulfilment. It means that in the birth, life, ministry, and death of Jesus, God was doing something which has ultimate significance for our lives and the life of all mankind. It means that either we come to terms with the historic Jesus and bring our lives into harmony with his, or we miss the path of life altogether. Thus I came to know Jesus, and thus many people know him — as the great revealer of God. But that is still not the best.

III Such knowledge by itself is not enough to make a real difference in our lives. By the time I was ordained I believed that I had a gospel to preach. I had read the New Testament and kept most of the information at my finger-tips. I had studied the great theologians and steeped my mind in their theories of the incarnation and the atonement. I knew all the facts, so I thought. Yet by themselves those facts seemed lifeless and powerless. It was as though I held a noble sword in my hand, but my hand was too weak to lift it. Something was still missing in my Christian development. What was it?

The awakening came in the early years of my ministry when I turned from the writings of the scholars to the writings of the saints and mystics. They knew about Jesus, but more than that — *they knew Jesus himself.* They spoke about him as though he were still alive and just as real to them as he was to the disciples in Galilee and Judea. Samuel Rutherford wrote to a friend from prison, "Jesus Christ came into my cell last night, and every stone flashed like a ruby." David Livingstone said that it was not he alone but he and Jesus who went tramping together through darkest Africa. I met some of these saints among the people to whom I ministered. While I spoke from the pulpit about a *man* who revealed God two thousand years ago, they spoke in their homes about a personal *friend* who called to see them yesterday.

So I went back to the New Testament to make certain that all those saints, ancient and modern, were not dreaming. For the first time I realized that the apostle Paul, who wrote much of the New Testament, though he lived at the same time and in the same part of the world, never met the historic Jesus. Yet Paul knew Jesus as intimately as Peter and John knew him. Travelling to Damascus to persecute the Christians, he saw a blinding light and heard a voice saying distinctly, "I am Christ whom you are persecuting" (Acts 9:5 RSV), and from that moment his life became an adventure in comradeship with the great revealer of God. Paul never refers to Jesus in the past tense. For him Christ is not only the friend of sinners who once said to a paralytic, "My son, your sins are forgiven" (Mark 2:5 RSV); he is the living Saviour who breaks the shackles of guilt here and now. Christ is not only the timeless teacher who showed us the way to live; he is the power within us who enables us to follow that way. Christ is not only the incarnate Son of God who reconciled us to God on the cross; he is the home of our souls, and if we live in him we are eternally at home with God.

It all has to do with the fact that Jesus rose from the dead. That was the great conviction that flooded the soul of Malcolm Muggeridge and inspired his heart-warming book, *Jesus Rediscovered*, that contains in his own words a digest of the gospel story so lucid and convincing that a real Christ, an alive Christ steps out of its pages. Mr Muggeridge believes that Christ is real and alive. He is sure of that because he met Christ on the road to Emmaus, the actual road in the Holy Land where he had been preparing some films for BBC television. He recalls the story of the two disciples walking that road on the first Easter evening and how they were joined by a stranger who showed himself to be their Saviour risen from the dead. Then he tells how he and his friend, walking the same road twenty centuries later and reading the gospel story, were joined by a third presence. He says, "I tell you that wherever they walk, and whoever the wayfarers, there is always this third presence ready to emerge from the shadows and fall in step along the dusty, stony way."[6]

Speaking personally, I cannot tell you the exact date of my own spiritual awakening. I can only say that at some point Jesus became very real for me. I found myself talking to him as naturally as I talk to the closest friends, confiding my problems, confessing my failures, asking him to forgive and help me. My ministry went beyond the attempt to propagate his teachings and tell what he had done and became an earnest effort to share in what he is doing. When I entered a sick room, I felt his presence beside me, and when I stepped into the pulpit, I felt his hand on my shoulder. My wife said that a look of radiant affection came into my eyes whenever I spoke the name of Jesus. No longer did I know only Jesus, the man of history, I felt that I knew the Christ of faith by personal experience; and that is how many Christians know him. But that is still not the best.

IV Such knowledge by itself does not do justice to the complete picture of Jesus. I had been in the ministry for several years before I came to know Jesus as he is portrayed in much of the New Testament. There was a time when I set myself to do a series of studies on the New Testament portraits of Jesus — the teacher portrayed in Matthew, the martyr in Mark, the healer in Luke, the high priest in Hebrews. When I consulted the earliest sermons recorded in the Acts of the Apostles I was struck by the fact that the disciples of Jesus did not look backward and paint this figure in the light of their past memories; they looked upward and forward and painted him in the glory of their present faith and future hope. They did not think of their master, as we might expect, in the associations of Galilee and Jerusalem; they thought of him in the majesty of heaven, seated at the right hand of God. I found that this same regal portrait dominated other parts of the New Testament — the letters of Paul and especially the Book of Revelation where Christ is shown as King of kings and Lord of lords whose kingdom will come in its fulness at the end of the age.

This is the Christ portrayed by the great tapestry in the new Coventry Cathedral. I confess I really don't like the tapestry; it does not strike me as a thing of beauty. The severe lines and the stark, garish colours, predominantly green, yellow, black, remind me of a coat of arms or an old school tie. Yet I admire the courage of the architect and the integrity of the artist in attempting to picture symbolically the highest stage in our knowledge of Christ. We have not grasped the final truth about Jesus until we know that the Man of Galilee, who revealed God in his life and death upon this earth and now fills the world with his risen presence, sits on the throne of the universe and rules over all history by the power of his cross and resurrection.

That is the truth symbolized by the event of Christ's ascension, of which there are two accounts in the New Testament. Luke tells us that, after the risen Lord had dwelt with his disciples for a period of time, after he had commissioned them for their work in the world, he led them out of Jerusalem to Bethany where he blessed them and then vanished from their sight (24:50-51). The account in Acts tells of his being lifted up by a cloud and of men in white robes telling the disciples that their Lord has ascended to heaven (1:9-11). If you go to Jerusalem today you can visit a small chapel on the Mount of Olives which reputedly marks the actual site of Christ's ascension. We do not know what happened there. The chapel is a symbol, and so is the event which it commemorates. What matters to us is the truth which the ascension proclaims, the triumphant truth of Christ living eternally in the glory of God the Father. That was the truth that burned like fire in the hearts of the disciples and sent them back to Jerusalem with great joy.

The knowledge of the kingly Jesus fills *our* hearts with great joy, and we need something to make us joyful these days. Science opens before our eyes a vast, expanding, seemingly soulless universe. Blind, irrational forces sweep across history like the choking sands of the desert. Theologians knock the props from beneath all that we have believed about God. What can we hang on to any more? We can hang on to this: that the power which holds this expanding universe together is the power that was present in a Bethlehem stable; the unseen purpose that controls the forces of history is the purpose of love that was made plain on Calvary's cross; the God who sits on the throne of eternity is the God who raised Jesus Christ from the dead. That is our highest knowledge of Jesus. Yet even that is not the best.

Then what *is* the best? Ask that question about any person. Let a man ask it about his wife. In which of her roles does he love her the most — as a friend, companion, partner, lover, cook, homemaker, the mother of his children? What an absurd question! Love does not atomize the beloved. It's not in any one of these roles but in all of them together that a wife endears herself to her husband. He loves her whole personality, all that she can be to him. So it is with our love for Christ. We don't choose among Christ teacher, revealer of God, personal Saviour, Lord of history. We love Christ for all that he can be to us. The best of Christ is his fullness. Why not the best?

WHY NOT CHRISTIAN COMMITMENT?

The theme "Why Not The Best?" is borrowed from the title of a book by Jimmy Carter which he wrote before he was elected President of the United States. He tells us that when he was a young naval officer he applied for the nuclear submarine program and was interviewed by Vice-Admiral Hyman Rickover whom he greatly admired. The Admiral asked, "How did you stand in your class at the Naval Academy?" With some pride Carter said, "Sir, I stood 59th in a class of 840." He expected praise. Instead came the question, "Did you do your best?" Carter was about to reply, "Yes sir," but he thought about it for a moment and replied honestly, "No sir, I didn't always do my best." After a long silence the Admiral said, "Why not?"

So President Carter called his book, *Why Not the Best?*[7] It's not a religious book, although the President is a deeply spiritual man. However, it poses a religious question, in fact, the fundamental question of Christian evangelism, more relevant than, "Are you saved?" Too much evangelism assumes that everybody is drowning and needs saving, whereas Christ addressed much of his ministry to people who could swim. He came not only to make bad people good but to challenge good people with the best. The church's question, as it confronts people with Christ, is essentially, "Why not the best?"

In the eighth chapter of the Acts of the Apostles we meet an admirable person who caught a glimpse of Christ and asked that question himself. He was a colourful character, a black man, the treasurer of the Queen of Ethiopia and therefore a person of considerable wealth and influence. Also he was a Gentile, one of the first Gentiles to become a Christian. His conversion happened under the influence of Philip, the first Christian evangelist, who had already proved himself to be a powerful preacher and healer. Philip was walking along the road south from Jerusalem when he saw this man sitting in his chariot and reading aloud from the fifty-third chapter of Isaiah. Although a Gentile, the Ethiopian was attracted to the Jewish religion because of its monotheism and high moral standards. He was returning home from a religious festival in Jerusalem. Philip accompanied him in his chariot and showed him that the ancient prophecy had been fulfilled in Jesus. When they came to a place of running water, the man himself said, "See, here is water! What is to prevent my being baptized?" (Acts 8:36 RSV).

He was really asking, "Why not the best?" He asked it as a good man who believed in God, read the Bible, said his prayers, and led a morally upright life. In that sense he represents many people in our secular society today. They have been condescendingly described as good pagans, but they are more than that. Some have the essential spirit of religious faith, they display fine Christian qualities, they attend church occasionally, they admire Jesus Christ — but they have never really confessed their faith in him and committed their lives to him. What can an act of commitment give them that they don't already have? What did it give to the Ethiopian who asked to be baptized because he believed that, although he had what was good, Christ offered him what was best?

I Commitment to Christ gave him *a new apprehension of God.* He had been reading the chapter in Isaiah which tells of a suffering servant of God, despised and rejected of men, who was put to death in a horrible way but whose death atoned for the sins of his people and brought them healing and salvation. When Philip asked, "Do you understand what you are reading?" the man replied, "How can I understand unless someone will give me the clue?" (NEB). Philip showed him that Christ on his cross was the suffering servant of God who gave up his life as an offering for sin and justified many by bearing their iniquities. That gave the man a new apprehension of God, as he saw what God had done for him and for all people. That was the best he had ever heard of God, and in offering to make a commitment of faith, he was really asking, "Why not the best?"

That's not to say that non-Christians know nothing about God. Some of them know a great deal — whether they are poets, mystics, adherents of other religions, or godly people who have the essential spirit of religious faith. It is not the purpose of Christian evangelism to persuade them that their faith is inferior and their knowledge of God incomplete. Philip didn't take that approach to the man in the chariot. He told him the good news of Jesus Christ, and the man responded in faith because he believed that Christ brought him closer to God than he had ever been before. Christ revealed God to him in a new way.

It is in this sense that we offer Christ as the best. We are not pleading for his so-called "uniqueness" which seems to be a problem to some people both outside and inside the church. A writer in *The Christian Century* stated that in our increasing contact with other religions "an insistence on the uniqueness of the historical Jesus can only be a hindrance." He added, "Christians should never have made a God out of Jesus. It is just too preposterous to believe that God gave her/his world-embracing love uniquely through Jesus."[8] He could be right, apart from the claims that Jesus made for himself and assuming that the primary task of the church is to make contact with other religions. But what if the church's mandate is to proclaim the gospel to people who have no religion? God may indeed have revealed himself in other ways, but Christ is still the best *we* know about God, and that's why we continue to tell about him. We are asking, Why not the best?

The best, however, is more than knowing about Christ. That will not bring us to a new apprehension of God. The best is an act of commitment such as the man made when he said, "What is to prevent my being baptized?" Some years ago J.H. Oldham wrote a book called *Life Is Commitment* which he addressed mainly to those people in society who have not found Christ but are unconsciously searching for him. He tells them frankly that religion differs radically from other forms of knowledge because it cannot be approached by the academic high-road alone. "There are some things in life," writes Dr. Oldham, "and they may be the most important things, that we cannot know by research or reflection, but only by committing ourselves. We must dare in order to know." He adds, "Life is full of situations to which I can respond not with part of myself but only with the commitment of my whole being."[9]

That is supremely true of Jesus Christ. It was true from the beginning. The twelve disciples gained great insight into Jesus on the road to Caeserea Philippi when he asked, "Who do you say that I am?" and Peter confessed, "You are the Christ, the Son of the living God." (Matt. 16:16 RSV). This response was so profound that, according to Jesus, it had to be inspired by God. In Mark's gospel that incident begins, "and *on the way* he asked his disciples . . ." (8:27) — a phrase which denotes something larger than a country road in Palestine. "On the way," Christ's way, people have always received a new apprehension of God. The deepest insights come to us not in the ivory tower of speculation but on the rough road, the way of Christian commitment. The Ethiopian put himself in the way of Christ. That was the best he could do, it is the best we can do.

II Commitment to Christ gave him not only a new apprehension of God but *an experience of rebirth*. Baptism in the name of Christ has always signified rebirth — first immersion, a burial with Christ; then coming up out of the water, a resurrection with Christ. The story does not say that Philip explained the theology of baptism. He simply told the good news of Jesus, and the man responded with an act of Christian commitment. There his old life ended, and there his new life began. He was born a second time.

Apart from religion, the experience of rebirth answers a great longing in the human heart. Who among us has not taken a good look at what he has made, or failed to make, of life and wistfully thought of what he would change, if he could go back to the beginning and make a fresh start? Who has not said, "If I had it to do over again," and wished that he did, in fact, have it to do over again? Who has not wanted to be a different person than he is now? Who has not longed to be reborn?

Spiritual rebirth has always been the aim, the result, and the miracle of evangelism. The whole story of Christianity can be gathered under the title of a book by Harold Begbie, *Twice-Born Men*. People have heard the good news of Jesus Christ, they have responded with an act of commitment, and they have become new creatures, living a new life to which the natural man can no more attain than a crawling thing can fly. They were not all sinners in the narrow sense. It wasn't to a sinful person that Jesus said, "Except a man be born again, he cannot see the kingdom of God" (John 3:3 KJV); it was to Nicodemus, a godly and righteous person who represents many people today.

A graduate student in a theological seminary said to one of the older professors, "I am convinced that many people in our churches need an experience of rebirth, and I should like to have it myself, but how do you do it?" The professor replied quietly, "*You* don't do it. God does it." The student shook his head and walked sadly away. He clung to the old illusion of self-salvation, the illusion of people who are always making new resolutions and fresh starts in the hope that each change of circumstance will change their personalities and give them an experience of rebirth. He failed to understand that we do not have the power to re-create life any more than we have the power to create it in the first place. Only a power from outside can release the power from within.

That power is Jesus Christ, the best that God has given us. "If any man be in Christ," writes Paul, "he is a new creature: old things are passed away; behold, all things are become new" (2 Cor. 5:17 KJV). Paul has been talking about the death and resurrection of Christ and how they represent the operation of God's grace and power in any person who becomes by faith a person in Christ. That happened to Paul — as Saul the Pharisee he had died with Christ on his cross; as Paul the apostle he had risen with Christ in his resurrection. What God did for Christ he does for Paul and for every person who identifies with Christ, believes in Christ, and commits himself to the way of Christ. God kills that person, kills his pride, egotism, ambitions, achievements, kills everything about him and buries him, sometimes in a grave of suffering and failure; then God raises that person, brings him to birth a second time, makes him a new creature with a new hope of achieving his appointed destiny.

That truth comes across from an old Dutch fable about three tulip bulbs named No, Maybe, and Yes. They lived at the bottom of a bulb tin, content to be round and fat and clothed in their silky, brown garments. When autumn came, they fell to discussing the destiny of tulip bulbs. No said, "I shall stay in my snug corner of the bin; I don't think there is any other life for tulip bulbs. Besides, I am satisfied with things as they are." And he rolled over in the corner to sleep the winter away. Maybe said, "I am not satisfied with things as they are; I feel something inside me which I must achieve and I believe that I can achieve it." So he squeezed and squeezed and squeezed himself, and finally rolled over in a fit of frustration. Yes said, "I have been told that we can do nothing of ourselves but that the good Lord will fulfil our destiny for us if we put ourselves in his power." One day a hand reached down into the bin groping for tulip bulbs. Yes gave himself to the hand and was buried in the cold earth throughout the long winter months. Meanwhile No and Maybe shrivelled away, but when spring came, Yes burst forth with all the richness and loveliness of new life.

It's a simple story, like many that Jesus told, but it illustrates a profound spiritual truth. We commit ourselves to Christ, as the Ethiopian did, we place our lives in his hand, and he gives us an experience of his own death and resurrection. We are born a second time. We start life all over again. That is the best we can do.

III Commitment to Christ gave the Ethiopian not only a new apprehension of God and an experience of rebirth but also *a complete dedication*. That's another word for commitment. The Christian who commits his life to Christ in baptism or confirmation, at an evangelistic mission or in the secret place of his own heart, is *really* putting himself in the hands of Christ. It means that his life is no longer his own. He now belongs to Christ as a slave belongs to his master. He is pledged to obey Christ, and his purpose is to serve Christ.

Christians are not the only people dedicated to a higher purpose than their own comfort and security. In all areas of life — in politics, education, science, medicine, labour, the home, and military service — we see magnificent examples of dedication. One of the most heroic came to light thirty years after the Second World War when a Japanese Lieutenant, who had been given up for dead, emerged from the Philippine jungles. He didn't know that the war was over and, when he made that discovery, he returned to his hideout to retrieve his sword which in an act of surrender he presented to the commander of the Philippine Air Force. He told newspapermen that he had not come out before because he had not received the order. His last order was to keep up guerilla warfare, and he intended to obey it, even if it meant staying in the jungle forever. His aged parents wept for joy when they learned that their son had been found. His brother laid hands on his shoulder and told him, "You did well." Christians are not the only dedicated people!

But Christians are the only people dedicated to Jesus Christ. Their dedication embraces not only their duty but the inmost thoughts, motives, purposes, and decisions of their lives. Napoleon caught that truth when someone asked him what he considered to be the secret of the attractive power of Christ. He said, "Well then, I will tell you. Across a chasm of eighteen hundred years, Jesus Christ makes a demand which is above all others difficult to satisfy. He asks for that which a philosopher may often seek at the hands of his friends, or a father of his children, or a bride of her spouse. He asks for the human heart. He will have it entirely to himself. He commands it unconditionally, and forthwith his command is granted. Wonderful! In defiance of time and space, the soul of man with all its powers becomes an annexation to the Empire of Christ."[10]

So it happened in the case of the Ethiopian treasurer. In an act of commitment he gave his heart unconditionally to Christ; and Christ gave focus to all his loyalties and gathered his life around one all-controlling purpose. After this admirable man came away from the place of his baptism he would never again have to ask himself, "What am I living for? What is the main business of my life?" He knew the answer. It was to serve Jesus Christ. We don't know his subsequent history, but we do know that if he remained faithful to the covenant of his baptism he would be committed to make every area of his life obedient to Christ. In every situation he would be controlled by one question: What does Christ want me to do? How can I best serve his purpose?

A man who made that kind of commitment was Sir Gordon Guggisberg, a distinguished officer of the First World War who served his country with dedication and loyalty. He later became governor of the Gold Coast of Africa. He was a strikingly handsome man, athletic and idealistic, but he felt no need of religion. On his shaving mirror he placed a card bearing the motto, "For God, for King, for Country." He said, "God meant nothing to me, the King meant a little, the Country everything." One day an earnest Christian said to him, "You love your country because you have served it all your life; you have taken every opportunity of seeing the King; but you have never sought or even wished to know God." The governor admired this forthright approach and asked how he could know God. The friend replied, "Some of us believe that Jesus of Nazareth knew more of God than any other man. We put aside some time each morning to study his thought of God and let his Father speak to us." Sir Gordon replied, "Damn it! I'll try. It's worth it if it's true." Six months later he became a committed Christian and through the years gave his life to the service of the Africans whom he loved — in fact, he became the most progressive governor in Africa. He founded a system of higher education for his people, and died a poor man because he had given all his money away.[11]

Even the strongest, most self-reliant, most dedicated person needs the complete dedication that an act of commitment to Christ can give him. After he has made that commitment, his strength and influence are transfigured and multiplied. A good person can do many wonderful things with his life, but the best he can do is commit his life to Jesus Christ. Why not the best?

WHY NOT THE CHURCH?

Suppose we *do* make an act of Christian commitment? Suppose we profess belief in a personal God, accept Jesus Christ as Saviour and Lord and respond to the gospel with a confession of faith that brings us to a new apprehension of God, an experience of rebirth, and the complete dedication of our lives to the kingdom of Christ? Where do we go from there?

Some people still need to be convinced that the best they can do, after responding positively to the gospel, is join the church. In 1966 Billy Graham conducted a crusade at Earlscourt Arena in London, England, where he preached powerful sermons that drew hundreds of decisions for Christ. As a minister in London at the time I followed up the decision cards that were sent to me but without much success. Many of the people whom I contacted could see no connection between being a Christian and being a member of the church, and some stated that they could be better Christians outside the church.

That's not typical of the Graham Crusades, which usually result in a great influx of new members into the churches. The reaction is similar to that on the Day of Pentecost when Peter preached a sermon that drew three thousand decisions for Christ. Lesslie Newbigin compares the events of Pentecost to a violent eruption of oil that bursts into flame and burns for many days before being brought under control. It has to be pumped through pipes and refineries, man-made channels, to its destination. What begins with a terrific display of power must settle down to a steady, mundane, but productive business.[12]

There was a display of power on the Day of Pentecost — a sound from heaven, the rush of mighty wind, tongues of fire, and the gospel of Christ proclaimed in a chorus of many languages. Then Peter preached his sermon. He told about Jesus and all the wonderful things that he did, how the authorities put him to death, how God raised him from the dead and made him Lord and Christ. It all had a terrific impact on the bystanders who felt that God had laid hold on them irresistibly and filled them with burning conviction. But they did a very ordinary thing about their new conviction — they joined the church. They realized that if their new and vital experience of God were to be more than a mere display of unharnessed spiritual energy, if it were to last and be productive, it must settle down and be directed through man-made channels to its destination. The Pentecost story concludes, ". . . there were added that day about three thousand souls. And they devoted themselves to the apostles' teaching and fellowship, to the breaking of bread and the prayers" (Acts 2:41,42 RSV). That was the best they could do, the best we can all do. Why not the best?

I   If we look more deeply into this story we shall discover three reasons why those new Christians immediately joined the church. First, they would feel a sense of indebtedness as they realized that their experience of Christ had originated within the church. Actually the experience happened in an upper room, the same room where Christ instituted the Last Supper and appeared after his resurrection to bring the gifts of peace and power and joy to his disciples. Those disciples had been his companions from the beginning. They had heard his teachings, witnessed his miracles, and shared his earthly ministry. In the upper room he commissioned them to continue his ministry, entrusted to them the issues of his kingdom, and promised to be with them always. They would be his church, his new corporate body in which he would live just as surely as he had lived in a fleshly body. People would find him there, as they did on the Day of Pentecost; they would come to know him and be related to him as in no other way.

There is an old and beautiful legend about Zacchaeus, the tax collector whom Jesus called down from the sycamore tree and to whose house he brought salvation (Luke 19:1–10). The legend says that in later years he used to rise early every morning and leave the house. His wife was curious to know where he went and what he did; so one morning she followed him. At the town well he lowered a bucket, filled it with water, went out through the city gates, and walked until he came to a sycamore tree. There, setting down the bucket, he began to gather and cast away the stones and branches and rubbish that lay about the foot of the tree. Having done that, he poured water on the roots and stood there in silence, gently caressing the trunk with his hands. When his amazed wife came out of her hiding place and asked what he was doing, Zacchaeus replied simply, "This is where I found Christ."

For nineteen centuries people have borne that same tender, affectionate witness concerning the church. Ask a Jerusalem Christian where he found Christ, and he would say, "I found him in an upper room in a company of Christian believers who devoted themselves to teaching and fellowship, to the breaking of bread and the prayers." Ask a modern Christian where he found Christ, and he would say, "I found him in a parish church where the pews were hard, the music atrocious, and the sermons dull, but where godly Sunday School teachers told me Bible stories I have never forgotten." In the 1960s when the anti-church syndrome was at its height, Elton Trueblood, the Quaker philosopher who had never been strong on institutional religion, wrote in his book *The Incendiary Fellowship,*

> Though I am as conscious as are most people of the inadequacies of the local church, and though I am sure that the church is not the building, I can never pass a little building devoted to Christ's cause without a sense of reverence and the utterance of a short prayer of thanksgiving.... Furthermore, I can never forget that, apart from the poor little fellowships in such poor little buildings, there isn't a chance in the world that I would be enlisted today in the cause of Christ.[13]

Another person will have a different story to tell. He may say, "I found Christ on a battlefield or in the pages of a book. I consider myself a Christian, though I never darken the door of a church." Even if that person's estimate of himself were true, he could not be a Christian unless someone at some time had darkened the door of a church. Whatever we possess of Christianity we owe to the church's influence. Christianity is Christ; but we could never have heard of Christ if the gospel had not been written and interpreted, proclaimed and transmitted through nineteen centuries of lived experience in the church. We can no more escape the church's influence than we can escape the influence of our parents. We are surrounded on every hand by traditions that came out of the church, by families whose roots are in the church, by ideas and institutions that were born of the church, and by men and women who believe in and serve the church. Apart from that direct or indirect influence there would be no Christianity in the world. To be sure, the church has no monopoly on Christ, but Christ lives supremely in his church, as he said that he would. That is the best that Christ has given us.

II There is a second reason why the men and women who felt the power of the Holy Spirit at Pentecost promptly joined the church. They believed that they needed the church. They knew that the church, being the source of their Christian experience, was also the soil in which that experience could grow, so they thrust their roots into the apostles' teaching and fellowship, the breaking of bread and the prayers.

Look at those four activities which have always been the distinctive features of the church's life. "They devoted themselves to the apostles' teaching." We still devote ourselves to the apostles' teaching. We recite the historic creeds — not because we understand them perfectly, but because they are rooted in the Bible and because they contain the body of Christian belief which has held the church together through the centuries. We listen to sermons, attend Bible classes, join discussion groups, and read books in order to study the creeds and learn what they mean for us, how they apply to our own lives and the life of the world today. We believe that we grow in faith by belonging to the community of faith.

They devoted themselves to the apostles' "fellowship." There was nothing theological about that; it was simply a case of meeting human need. Man is a social being. On all levels of life he admits the need of human fellowship. He works more happily and efficiently when he works alongside other people. He likes to share his interests in books and music and flowers. He laughs more heartily at television comedy when someone laughs beside him. He has the same social need in religion. A few exceptional Christians may be able to live the Christian life in isolation, but most of us are like logs burning in a fire. We sustain the spiritual glow only in the warm, strengthening company of other Christians.

They devoted themselves to "the breaking of bread and the prayers." The first Christians always seemed to be at a prayer meeting, communicating with God or listening to a sermon in which God communicates with them. It all had to do with the fact that they saw Christianity not as men's enterprise but as God's; therefore they lived close to God and opened their lives to his guidance and power. That is why the public worship of God is still the central event in the church's life. Christians worship because they need to worship. They believe with Archbishop William

Temple that to worship "is to quicken the conscience by the holiness of God, to feed the mind with the truth of God, to purge the imagination by the beauty of God, to open the heart to the love of God, and to devote the will to the purpose of God."

The fourth distinguishing feature of the church's life is a particular mode of worship — the sacrament of Holy Communion. They devoted themselves to "the breaking of bread." Christians believe that the Communion is a re-enactment of the gospel, a visual presentation of the life, death, and resurrection of Christ. We believe that Christ is present and that through the bread and wine he imparts himself to us as in no other way. We believe that the sacrament is necessary to our growth in the Christian life.

A recent convert to Christianity, who joined the church for the same reasons as the early converts, was the late E.F. Schumacher, an economist who wrote a book entitled *Small Is Beautiful: Economics As If People Mattered*[14] which has sold more than a million copies worldwide. Schumacher believes that the only answer to the world's economic problems is for each of us to put his own inner house in order. It troubles him that most people in the West are suffering today through what he calls an anti-Christian trauma. He went through it himself for twenty years. About 1950 he stumbled across a book about Buddhism which affected him profoundly, yet he realized that if he went around England passing himself off as a Buddhist, he would be assuming that his religion was right and everybody else's was wrong. Instead he followed the advice of Mahatma Gandhi who said to his Christian friends from the West, "As far as your religion is concerned, stay at home." So he stayed at home spiritually; he became a Christian. He also joined the church because, as he says, "If everyone else around me who is a Christian has a need for a church, am I really so different and better that I don't?" He says that he gets a great deal out of the church, especially the ritual, and adds, "Even if I could sustain a free-floating spirituality, which I can't, my children surely couldn't, and it's important to me that religion be a family affair." He is saying, in effect, that a person can really be the best kind of Christian inside the church.

III There must have been a third reason why those early Christians on the Day of Pentecost identified themselves with the church. Surely they believed not only that they needed the church but that the church needed them. Within the church they had been introduced to Christ, within the church their experience of Christ would grow and their obedience to Christ would find expression. If they were to obey Christ and serve him in any significant way, they must do so through the visible structure which Christ himself had established.

You hear people saying that they believe in Christianity but not in the church. That's rather like saying that they believe in education but not in schools, in music but not in orchestras. Any concerned person who burns with conviction on a social issue and wants to do something about it knows that he cannot be a one-man crusade. He has to work through social structures and identify himself with the fellowship of those who share his concern and are in a position to act politically. The socialist will join a political party or a labour union; otherwise he will be like a piccolo player attempting to reproduce by himself the glory of Beethoven's Fifth Symphony. That's why concerned Christians join the church. They may join political parties and labour unions — and the more Christians in those organizations, the better! But Christians also join the church; they do so because the church is the visible and historic structure through which the Spirit of Christ operates in the world.

Think of some of the things that the church has done and is doing which no Christian individual could undertake by himself. To be sure, the church as an institution has made mistakes and sometimes hurt rather than helped society, but read the whole story and ask yourself if any single institution has played a more decisive role in the impulse to human freedom and dignity, the challenging of ignorance, the relief of suffering, the conquest of disease, the growth of humanitarian concern for the weak, helpless and destitute; the inspiration to great art and literature, architecture and music; the enlarging of personal horizons; the incentive to more sensitive and concerned moral living; the stabilizing of the inner lives of millions of people through the ages and around the world; the fostering of prophetic attacks by determined minorities on such giant evils as race prejudice, economic exploitation, and war.

The church today is far from perfect, and no people are more aware and ashamed of that than its most loyal members. Yet they remain loyal because they can imagine our society as it would fast become if all the churches had to close their doors for lack of support. They can see a society deprived of its major character-building agency, the one institution that exists to remind people that God is sovereign and that we are subject to his laws. They see a society deprived of the well-spring of human charity, the one institution that exists to kindle in the hearts of people a sense of love and responsibility for their fellows. They see a society deprived of its great source of hope, the one institution that exists to remind people that even when they lose control of the world, God does not lose control. They see a society deprived of its great reconciling power, the one institution that exists to reconcile people to God and therefore to one another. All of which prompted one of America's leading theologians to say,

> Now I happen to believe that in cold, realistic, practical terms, the best hope for world civilization lies in the Christian Church. Despite its divisions, its stuffiness, its slowness, its enslavement to nationalistic prejudices, social conservatism, and rigid dogma, the church is mankind's most effective instrument for restoring mutual confidence, for instilling contrition, for allaying anxiety, and for opposing fanatical will-to-power.[15]

That's what all of us who are Christians happen to believe. That's why we eagerly invite others to join us in the church. We believe, as the early Christians did, that we owe a debt to the church, we need the church, and the church needs us. We believe that the church is the spiritual home where we came to know Christ, the soil in which our experience of Christ can grow, the instrument through which our obedience to Christ can find expression. We believe that the church is the purest, noblest, bravest, tenderest, most tenacious, universal and redemptive institution in history and in the world today. We believe that the church is the best that God has given us for serving and being served by the gospel of Jesus Christ. Why not the best?

WHY NOT THE RESURRECTION?

When I was a young minister I once addressed the students at an Anglican theological seminary in Western Canada. My subject, for some reason, was the Christian belief in immortality. I spoke of the instinct for immortality which the Creator has implanted in his children, an instinct that will surely not deceive us. I spoke about the universality of this belief, its acceptance by all civilizations and by intellectual giants of every age. I added the moral consideration that only on the basis of hope in a future life do the injustices and inequalities of this life make sense. I thought I was building up a rather convincing case when a student suddenly jumped to his feet and said, "But sir, the church accepts all of those arguments."

I have often wondered what became of that young man who seemed to imply that I was wasting my time. He is probably a bishop now. I resented his interruption then, but now I realize that he was teaching me more than I taught him. What he really meant was that the church has something better to offer than philosophical arguments for a general belief in immortality. But the church offers a stronger hope than immortality; it offers a particular personal hope of resurrection. That is the best that the church has to offer; and that student was saying, "Why not the best?"

The Apostle Paul said the same thing when he wrote to the Christians in Corinth, "Christ has been raised from the dead, the first fruits of those who have fallen asleep" (1 Cor. 15:20 RSV). When Paul left Corinth and moved to Ephesus he received reports that some of the Corinthians were having doubts about their new faith. They were not rejecting it altogether, just watering it down to a point where it made no real difference in their lives and offered them no comfort, no hope, no incentive to live morally. For example, they had fallen back on their old pre-Christian belief in the immortality of the soul and settled for it as though they had never heard the gospel of Jesus Christ. Paul preaches that gospel in the fifteenth chapter of his first Corinthian letter. He begins with the story of Easter and a list of the resurrection appearances of Jesus. Then he says, in effect, "My friends, you are living on the wrong side of Easter. God has given us something better than the hope of immortality; he has given us the hope of resurrection; and there is a world of difference between the two. As Christ was dead, and God raised him from the dead; so, when we die, if we are in Christ, God will raise us from the dead. That is the best hope that God has given us. Why settle for less than the best?"

Why indeed? When we set the two hopes side by side we see that whereas immortality is a hope that the *soul* of a person survives death, resurrection hopes that the *person himself* will survive.

There is nothing very comforting about the belief in immortality. It is vague and general and can mean a variety of things. It can mean that while the body returns to earth, the spirit returns to God and is lost in God as a drop of water is lost in the boundless ocean. Immortality can mean simply that a person lives on in his children. It does not mean that for which the hearts of his children hunger and thirst — the hope that the person himself lives on, the hope that he is still alive, still belongs to them, still loves them, the hope that they will see him again.

The distinction that our funeral liturgies make between the body and the soul has no basis in the Bible. Scripture sees man in his wholeness. If a man dies, the whole man dies; if a man lives, the whole man lives. Man is a single being in life and in death. The very word "body" in the Bible means personality; and the resurrection of the body means that the personality, the person himself, the whole person will live again after he dies.

That's what happened on Easter Day and that's why the disciples were so ecstatic with joy. It was a real Jesus who emerged from the tomb, the same Jesus whom they had seen crucified, dead, and buried. He met them in the garden and called them by name. He walked with them on the road and explained the meaning of the scriptures. He sat down at table and ate with them and gave thanks to God for the meal. He came to them in the upper room and displayed the wounds in his hands and side. He met them on the shore and showed them where to catch fish after they had toiled all night and caught nothing. Every appearance, every word, every gesture convinced the disciples that after his death Jesus was still alive and real, still the same familiar friend whom they had known and loved and followed in the days of his flesh.

A few years ago a theological scholar in the United States died at the untimely age of forty-six. Among those who mourned was a three-year-old boy, the playmate of his little daughter. He felt perplexed and indignant until his mother told him that Wendy's daddy was with God. Then he replied in tones of infinite acceptance and understanding, "Oh! Then he's still real."[16] The gospel of resurrection is a hope that after you die you are still real, still alive, still recognizable, still you. That is the best hope that God has given us.

II We can go further and say that while the immortality of the soul promises *more* of the same thing, the resurrection of the body points to *something new*.

I have a friend who believes strenuously in re-incarnation. Not only so, but he tries to evangelize everyone else. He thinks that one chance to live a full, rich, useful life on this earth is not enough and that we should come back and keep coming back until we learn to do the job properly.

It always surprises my friend when someone says, "But I don't want to come back to the same mortal grind. I don't want to go around in circles to endless infinity. I want to go on to something new." The resurrection gospel promises that when we have finished with this mortal grind we shall, in fact, go on to something new. We shall not continue living on the same level but will rise to a higher level, an order of life with dimensions unknown in this life, experiences and opportunities of which our earth-bound minds cannot even dream. We shall exchange this old, broken-down body, not as we exchange a car for another one like it that will also be old and broken-down in a few years, but for a new body that will not be prone to the accidents and depreciations of space and time.

That's what happened to Jesus in his resurrection. The disciples did not recognize him at first. They mistook him for a gardener, a stranger, a ghost. He had a body, but a different body, no longer restrained by the limitations of earthly existence. It passed through locked doors, it materialized on the Emmaus Road, it vanished into air on the Mount of Olives; and when Paul saw it on the road to Damascus, it appeared to him in a blaze of blinding light.

Writing to the Corinthians, Paul says, "But you may ask, how are the dead raised? In what kind of body?" He answers, "How foolish! The seed you sow does not come to life unless it has first died." (1 Cor 15:35,36 NEB). That is a fact of nature. A seed dies in the earth. That is the end of its body as a seed. But God gives it a new body, a new, more beautiful existence as a plant, not in the dark earth but in the warm sunlight. A water beetle dies on the shore of a lake. That is the end of its body as a beetle. But out of its cracked shell comes a gorgeous dragonfly, exploring a wonderful new world and darting in an instant over space which a short time before would have taken it months to crawl. "So it is," writes Paul, "with the resurrection of the dead." If the Creator has worked such wonders with the lowliest of his creatures, what must he have in store for the human spirit! That is the best hope that God has given us.

III We can go still further and say that while the immortality of the soul is a generally accepted belief, the resurrection of the body is *a distinctively Christian belief.*

Most cultures and civilizations have believed in some form of life beyond the grave. The Greeks in ancient Corinth argued, as many people argue today, that man by his very nature is immortal. The physical side of him may decompose like a fallen tree, but man has a spiritual side which is independent of change and decay. "John Brown's body lies a-mouldering in the grave, but his soul goes marching on."

The New Testament does not deny the general belief in immortality, but neither does it affirm that man has a built-in capacity for survival beyond death. One fact dominates the life of man on this earth, and Paul articulates it when he says in this same chapter of his first Corinthian letter, "As in Adam all die." By the word "Adam" he means everything human, everything earthly, everything created; he means man himself, his history, his language, his institutions, his world, his racial solidarity. Over Adam hangs the inevitable sentence of death. Adam comes to an end, he passes out of existence, he ceases to be, he dies.

Jesus himself, insofar as he shared the nature of the old Adam, died on Calvary's Cross. The disciples were very sure of that. Nor did they ever say that Jesus was immortal, implying that while his body rotted in Joseph's sepulchre, his soul went marching on. They accepted the evidence of what their eyes told them — that Jesus was dead and everything about him was dead. There was no life left in him, no possibility of life unless God, the source of life, breathed life into him a second time. That's what God did; and it was the only conclusion the disciples could reach when they saw Jesus alive after he had been pronounced dead. Peter proclaimed it on the Day of Pentecost: "But God raised him up, having loosed the pangs of death, because it was not possible for him to be held by it" (Acts 2:24 RSV).

Here is the precise hope that the gospel holds out to us — not that we shall survive death, but that God by his grace and power will raise us from the dead. That hope derives from the very genius of Christianity, which is a religion predicated not on what man does for himself but on what God in his infinite grace has done for man. The general belief in the immortality of the soul places its trust in man; it says that we shall live beyond the grave because we are incapable of dying. The particular Christian belief in the resurrection of the body places its trust in God; it says that we shall live beyond the grave because God in his mighty love and loving might raises us from death to life. That is the best hope that God has given us.

IV We can take one more step and say that while the immortality of the soul costs nothing, the resurrection of the body comes at *the cost of obedience to Jesus Christ.*

Is it not strange how the most worldly people, as they approach the end of the journey, get a hankering to believe in immortality? Not that they fear the prospect of dying. It is the *nothingness* that they dread, the threat of non-being, of ceasing to exist and of ending up as a pinch of dust or ashes. Mark Twain, the humourist who became a cynic in later years, confessed to a friend, "I can't understand it. I've successfully exploded every possible argument for an after-life, and in spite of that, I fully expect there to be one."

It would be nice to say to Mark Twain, "Yes, there is an after-life, and we are all going to it. Let's look one another up when we get there." It would be nice to believe that every person graduates from the school of life whether or not he passes the examinations. But we have to read the New Testament very carefully at this point. It is crystal clear that Jesus, the "pattern-man," had to pass the examinations. As Paul says, it was because Jesus humbled himself and became obedient unto death, even death on a cross, that God highly exalted him and gave him a name which is above every name (Phil. 2:5–11). The resurrection was God's verdict upon his Son's perfect obedience. Therefore, if Christ has been raised from the dead, the first fruits of those who have fallen asleep, what was true for Christ must be true for us, and our resurrection must come at the cost of our obedience to him.

That is why the hope of the gospel makes sense only to a committed Christian. Only the person who lives with Christ on earth looks forward to living again with Christ in heaven. Only that person has a hope of heaven. Others are not excluded; they exclude themselves. The man who cares not a rap for the things that Christ cares for; who seldom takes a moment to worship Christ or understand him or talk with him in prayer; who is engrossed in the material things of life and has in him little or nothing of love for his fellows or concern for Christ's kingdom — that man does not look forward to heaven, because he would find heaven, as Christians conceive of it, to be one hell of a place.

So we return to the seminary student and we say to him, "You are right, young man. The gospel offers no arguments for immortality; rather it offers a hope that God who raised Christ from the dead will raise us with Christ if we are obedient to him; and it calls us to believe in Christ and trust him, follow him, and accept him as Saviour and Lord. That is the best that God has given us. Why not the best?

The Best
is the Greatest

AN EXAMPLE OF GREAT FAITH

The new sub-theme "the best is the greatest" derives from those few occasions in the gospel story when Jesus used the word "great." In Luke 7:2-10 he used it to pay tribute to a person's faith. That person was an obscure character who played a very small part in the New Testament drama, making only one brief appearance on the stage. He was not a disciple of Jesus, not a friend of Jesus, not even a Jew. He was a Roman centurion, an officer of the army that occupied the country of the Jews, therefore an enemy of the Jews. We might compare him to a German officer in occupied Poland or Norway during the Second World War.

We have a certain image of these Roman centurions, usually formed by sources outside the Bible. We think of them as the tough guys of the Roman army — which they sometimes were, although they could also be sensitive and sympathetic. Here, for example, in the city of Capernaum is a centurion concerned about his slave who was critically ill. In the Roman Empire you treated a sick slave with less compassion than you treated a sick horse; you let him die, perhaps even had him put to death. In this case, however, the gospel says, "Now a centurion had a slave who was dear to him." (RSV). He cared about his slave, grieved over his illness and wanted him to get well.

Another impression we have of Roman centurions is that they were all pagans who ridiculed religion as a barbarous superstition. There may have been those who fitted that description. Yet we know that some centurions responded positively to the preaching of John the Baptist (Luke 3:14). One of the first Gentiles to become a Christian was Cornelius, a centurion in Caeserea who received Peter into his own home (Acts 10:1vv). Of the centurion in Capernaum the Jews said to Jesus, "He loves our nation, and he built us our synagogue." In Capernaum today, the guide will show you the ruins of a first-century synagogue and tell you that it was originally the gift of the Roman officer who commanded the military garrison in that city.

But that was not the centurion's greatest claim to fame. This man stands out in the gospel story as being one of only two people, both Gentiles, whose faith Jesus praised as "a great faith." The other was a

Canaanite woman who pleaded with him to heal her demented daughter and who pressed her case with such indiscourageable trust that Jesus said to her, "O woman, great is your faith" (Matt. 15:21 RSV). The centurion pleaded with Jesus to heal his sick slave, and he pressed his case in such a way that Jesus said concerning him, "I have not found so great faith, no, not in Israel" (KJV). He stands before us as an example of great faith. What did he do to deserve that supreme tribute from Jesus? Of what did his great faith consist?

I   It consisted mainly in the fact that *he turned to Jesus for help.* That might be an obvious thing for a Christian to do but it was not obvious for the centurion. This man was an officer in the army of the Roman Empire, an army that ruled the world, and he was supposed to represent the superiority and self-sufficiency of Rome. He was supposed to believe that there was nothing that Rome could not do. For such a person to throw himself on the mercy of an itinerant Jewish faith-healer must have seemed absurd. Certainly he would have to overcome his own personal pride.

Faith still consists in turning to Jesus for help; and if that seemed absurd two thousand years ago, it is even more so today. Jesus lived in a relatively simple world, while our world is complex, sophisticated, and apparently self-sufficient. We have come to believe that there is nothing we cannot do. What help can a generation that travels faster than the speed of sound possibly get for its problems from a Palestinian peasant who travelled into Jerusalem on the back of a borrowed donkey? Does he even understand our problems?

In one of his books Louis Evans answers that question by telling a true parable. He recalls that during the First World War the French General Galliene devised a scheme to save the city of Paris, but first he had to obtain permission from General Foch. For security reasons he came to his superior's camp disguised in an old-fashioned, worn-out French uniform, looking so nondescript in his ridiculous outfit that a junior officer, without waiting for an explanation, ordered him out of camp. Later the officer told General Foch of the visitor and said that his name was Galliene. Foch exploded when he heard about this undiplomatic treatment of a great General, but the aide protested, "Who would take seriously an old man dressed up like that?" "That man," retorted Foch, "had a plan that could save the city of Paris and the lives of a million men." Commenting on the incident, Evans goes on to say, "There comes into our besieged world a Galilean with a plan that could save any city and far more than a million men. He comes in the outmoded garb of the first century. . . . Men often doubt that he could meet our contemporary needs, but he is 'the same yesterday, today and forever'."[17] To believe that and turn to him for help is the essence of faith.

The centurion turned to Christ in a time of personal crisis. It happened to be the illness of his servant but it might have been the breakdown of his own health, the collapse of his marriage, the loss of his job, the death of a child, the treachery of a friend, or the shame of moral failure. He reached a point where he confessed a need which neither Rome nor any other human power could meet, and he turned to Christ because he believed that only Christ could meet that need. That's what faith is all about. It is not exclusively a crisis measure. The spiritual needs are there all the time just as our need for food and drink, shelter and human love are there all the time. Every day of our lives we need the help of Christ to comfort us in sorrow, keep us faithful in duty, loyal in relationships, poised in trouble, and calm under stress. Faith is turning to Christ for help, though we may have to overcome our pride in order to get to him.

Charles Colson, the Watergate conspirator who spent a year in prison, wrote a book called *Born Again* in which he tells how he overcame his pride and turned to Christ for help. He had been the white-haired boy of the White House, Special Counsel to the President, Nixon's hatchet man. There was nothing he couldn't do. Then suddenly everything fell apart, and he found that he couldn't handle it any more. He went to see a friend, Tom Phillips, who talked to him about his soul and read from a book by C.S. Lewis who spoke of pride as a spiritual cancer, the complete anti-God state of mind. Then Phillips prayed with him. "Lord," he said, "we pray for Chuck and his family, that you might open his heart and show him the light and the way." God answered that prayer marvellously and mightily. He brought Charles Colson to a point of saying, "Lord Jesus I believe you. I accept you. Please come into my life. I commit it to you."[18] That is the first step of faith.

II The centurion's faith consisted in the fact that he turned to Jesus for help. Even more, it consisted in *the humility of his approach to Jesus*. To begin with, he did not come directly but sent the elders of the synagogue to intercede for him. The gospel writer says, "And when they came to Jesus, they besought him earnestly, saying, 'He is worthy to have you do this for him, for he loves our nation, and he built us our synagogue'." In response to that earnest appeal Jesus went with them to the centurion's house. Before he arrived, however, the centurion sent friends to Jesus with the message, "Lord, do not trouble yourself, for I am not worthy to have you come under my roof; therefore I did not presume to come to you."

The centurion knew quite well that a strict Jew, especially a rabbi, was forbidden by the religious law to enter the house of a Gentile, and presumably he was showing his respect for that law. Yet surely we can read a deeper meaning into his humble approach to Jesus. He was saying, in effect, "I am an outsider. I don't belong. I have no claim upon you, and you are under no obligation to help me, but I am appealing to you nevertheless." He had the spirit of the Canaanite woman whom Jesus tested by saying, "It is not fair to take the children's bread and throw it to the dogs," and who delighted his heart by her quick reply, "Yes, Lord, yet even the dogs eat the crumbs that fall from their master's table." The centurion was appealing for the crumbs.

Even in our own time this humble approach to Jesus is the sign of a great faith that Christ will help us whether or not we think that we qualify for his help. The greatest obstacle that deters any person from turning to Christ is a sense of his own unworthiness. He may not confess it openly. He may try to camouflage it with a smokescreen of pride and unbelief and self-sufficiency, but deep down he is saying to himself, "Why should Christ help me? What have I ever done for him? I haven't even been to church for years." Or he may say, "How can I expect Christ to do anything for me after the life I have lived?" As a pastor I offered to pray with a hospital patient who stopped me dead by saying, "I have never been a religious man, so don't make me a hypocrite now." I tried to explain to him that if Christ helped only religious people or if we had to deserve the help of Christ, none of us would have a right to pray.

The truth is that we have no more claim upon Christ than a certain man had upon Edmund Campion, the English Jesuit who was thrown into Tyburn prison and sentenced to be executed. On the day before his execution he had an amazing visitor. The spy, who had betrayed him and who knew his own life to be in peril from the vengeance of old friends, staggered into the cell behind a jailer and begged to be forgiven. Campion, weak from torture and facing death, freely and fully forgave him. Still the traitor lingered. Would the gracious father do more? Would he help him to escape from the fury of his pursuers? Without a word of rebuke Campion gave him a letter of introduction to a nobleman in Germany who would accept his services.[19]

That man exercised a great faith, an audacious faith. Although he was the last person in the world who had a right to expect help from Campion, he turned to the victim of his treachery because no other person in the world could help him. With the same faith we turn to Christ, believing that no other person in the world can help us, and believing that his motive for helping us lies not in our worthiness but in our need and in his grace. The clearest statement of that faith occurs in the fifth chapter of Paul's letter to the Romans: "While we were yet helpless, at the right time Christ died for the ungodly." He goes on to say, "Why, one will hardly die for a righteous man — though perhaps for a good man one will dare even to die." Then he adds, "But God shows his love for us in that while we were yet sinners Christ died for us" (vv.6-8 RSV). He died for us who betrayed him, the sinners who crucified him, the people least worthy to receive the outpouring of his grace upon the Cross. To turn to him for help, pleading his grace upon the cross, is the essence of a great faith.

III The centurion's faith reached its highest level when he recognized the *divine authority of Jesus*. As a soldier he knew all about authority. He lived under it and exercised it. He obeyed his superior officers, and his men obeyed him; and he saw at once that Jesus was a person who commanded obedience. Therefore he said, "I did not presume to come to you. But say the word, and let my servant be healed. For I am a man set under authority, with soldiers under me: and I say to one, 'Go', and he goes; and to another, 'Come', and he comes; and to my slave, 'Do this', and he does it."

That's what made Jesus marvel and evoked his word of praise, "I have not found so great faith, no, not in Israel." The centurion's great faith manifested itself in his recognition of the authority of Jesus, authority over illness, disease, evil, and death. He believed that with one word of command, even a long distance away, Jesus could heal his sick slave. That's what devout Jews did not recognize. Jesus had not found that faith even in the religious community of Israel. The religious leaders would later ask him, "By what authority are you doing these things?" (Mark 11:28 RSV). But here was a man outside the religious community who knew by what authority Jesus was doing these things, who instinctively recognized the power of God in Jesus and turned to him with complete faith in that power. Jesus not only praised his faith but responded to it. When the centurion's friends returned to the house, they found that the slave had recovered.

It is not enough to say that Christ *will* help us when we turn to him in our needs; we have to believe that he *can* help us, that he has power and authority to help us. Many people do not believe that. They say their prayers with less faith than they purchase a lottery ticket, believing that they have as much chance of being answered as they have of being struck by lightning. They are like the folk in Jesus' home town of Nazareth where it was said that "he did not do many works there because of their unbelief" (Matt. 13:58 RSV). Their unbelief blocks the divine power of Jesus, closes his means of access into their lives. The irony of it is that, though he praised the centurion's great faith, he does not demand a great faith as the condition of all that he can do for us. He told the disciples that even a small faith, like a grain of mustard seed, could open a situation to a more-than-human power (Luke 17:6).

Some years ago the *Reader's Digest* told a story of great faith. It concerned a man named Bob Stout whose head was critically injured in a train crash. A surgeon agreed to operate but made it clear that the chances were slim. On Sunday morning a nurse telephoned the pastor at the Methodist Church and said, "Mrs Stout is the only person in the world who thinks her husband will live. She keeps saying, 'I have put my trust in Christ'." Something prompted the pastor to interrupt the service that morning and invite the congregation to pray for Bob Stout. In his prayer he pictured Jesus as long ago he went about the earth touching the sick and healing them. Then he pictured the patient in hospital and said, "Master, we ask you to lay your hand on Bob's head and heal him." When he finished the prayer he noticed that the hands of his watch pointed to 11.20. After the service his telephone rang. It was Mrs Stout telling him that there was no need for the operation, her husband was going to recover, he had come out of the coma and opened his eyes. The minister asked, "Does anyone know what time it was when Bob first opened his eyes?" "Yes," she replied, "11.20".

That is an example of great faith, and it need not be reserved for a train crash. It can be the normal habit of life, a permanent posture in our relationship with God. Our whole life can be a turning to Christ, in spite of our unworthiness, a reaching out for help not only in crisis but in routine, not only to be picked up when we fall but to be kept from falling, not only to overcome our weakness but to perfect our strength and achieve our potential as children of God. There must be many of God's children who live from day to day in such a quiet, consistent faith that Jesus says, "I have not found so great faith, no, not in Israel."

CHRIST IS GREATER THAN RELIGION

One of the great experiences in my life happened on a bitterly cold morning in January 1965 when I attended the funeral of Sir Winston Churchill. I did not join the favoured few in St Paul's Cathedral but got up well before dawn and joined the thousands of mourners who lined the streets of London, many of whom had waited there all night. We watched the limousines that brought the mighty of the earth to pay their tribute. We heard the slow drum beat of the military bands playing the music of sorrow. Heading the procession was a single line of Royal Air Force veterans, the remnants of those "few" to whom Churchill had said that so many owed so much. At the end came the gun carriage, bearing the body of the great statesman, drawn by men of the Royal Navy. As it passed by, a deep hush settled upon the crowd, and one could sense the spirit of the man calling from the soul of the nation the greatness that he had called during the dark days of war. The occasion, the procession, the crowds, the cathedral, the VIPs, receded into the background. Something greater than all of them was there.

Our theme is greatness — measured not by human standards but by the standards of Jesus who was very sparing in the use of that word. He applied it once to himself when he said to the Pharisees, *"I tell you, something greater than the temple is here"* (Matt. 12:6 RSV). That must have fallen on their ears like blasphemy. To faithful Jews throughout the world there was nothing greater than the temple in Jerusalem. It was the focal point of their religion, the place of God's presence. God dwelt there in the holy of holies which only one person, the high priest, could enter, one day a year. The temple was so great that its priests were allowed even to break the sabbath laws. Jesus reminded the Pharisees of that fact when they rebuked his disciples for breaking those laws; then he spoke of something greater than the temple. He spoke of himself, the true holy of holies, in whom dwelt all the fullness of the eternal God. As the incarnate Son of God he superseded the temple, its priests, liturgies, and traditions, and all the institutions and regulations of religion.

Christ is greater than religion, just as the spirit of Sir Winston Churchill was greater than the historic and impressive occasion of his own funeral. No occasion, no institution, no religion is big enough, strong enough, lasting enough to contain the spirit of Christ. He bursts those man-made containers as he burst the sepulchre on Easter Day. The Bible is our tangible authority on the life, ministry, and teachings of Christ on earth, but Christ himself is greater than the Bible. Theology is our thought about Christ and our experience of Christ formulated into creeds, but Christ himself is greater than theology. Our worship through prayers, hymns, anthems, sermon, and sacrament, is a means of communion with Christ, but Christ himself is greater than worship. The church through nineteen centuries has been, as Paul described it, the body of Christ, the human dwelling in which he lives and through which he works, but Christ himself is greater than the church.

When Christ says, "I tell you, something greater than the temple is here," we must listen to him and believe him if we want to understand the purpose of evangelism. Much that goes by the name of evangelism simply represents an attempt by one group of people to sell their particular brand of religion to another group of people, but Christianity is not a brand of religion; it is Jesus Christ, and he is greater than all religion. The only valid purpose of evangelism is to hold up Jesus Christ, that people may see him as they have never seen him before and perhaps respond to him as they have never responded before.

I We must hold him up as *a fact of history*. Not that anyone doubts the historicity of Jesus, except perhaps Bertrand Russell who wrote in one of his books, "Historically it is quite doubtful whether Christ ever existed at all, and if he did, we do not know anything about him."[20] That statement surely proves that when a mathematician turns to biblical scholarship, his judgment is not infallible. To hold up Christ as a fact of history means reminding ourselves that our faith had its roots not in the visions and philosophies of men but in an historical event that happened at a specific time and place, a human drama that was enacted on the stage of history. At the centre of that drama was a man who lived, died, and rose from the dead, a man to whom people responded in such a way that the drama has never ended and shows no signs of ending.

Someone has said, "After Jesus Christ lived and died in it, the world could never be the same again. A new and vital energy entered the stream of human life." Nineteen centuries after his birth even the secular world cannot ignore the fact that there once lived a man named Jesus of Nazareth. There is the church to remind us, and the Bible, and a whole realm of art, architecture, literature, and music. There are the lives of the saints, a magnificent tradition of unselfish devotion and service. There is a civilization which is influenced to a far greater degree than we realize by Christ's standards and principles. It is simply not possible to tell the story of the past two thousand years and leave Jesus Christ out. To ignore him is to ignore not only a fact but *the* fact of history.

Look at it this way. For centuries the historical drama follows an unvarying pattern, with one scene substantially the same as another. Suddenly the curtain drops, the old drama ends, and a new drama begins. An event happens that changes everything and affects every man, woman, and child on the face of the earth, the generations alive and the generations yet unborn. Such an event was the atomic bomb — a fact of history which affects everybody, and which we ignore at our peril. So we regard Jesus Christ — a fact of history, an event that bisected history and started the human drama all over again. We ignore him at our peril, because he is the only answer, God's answer to the atomic bomb and to all other human schemes and inventions that threaten the future of mankind upon this earth.

A person who came to terms with that fact was Arthur Compton, one of the six scientists assigned by President Roosevelt to create the first atomic bomb. He wrote an article describing their various reactions when the experiment proved successful and they realized that a power that would change the course of history had been released. He said that he himself felt a sense of gratitude to God for another of his great gifts. He knew that it was a gift that put a big question mark over man's future, but about one thing there could be no question — that life on this earth could never be the same again. Wrote Dr Compton, "Man must now go the way of Jesus or perish."

The point is that we *can* go the way of Jesus and *not* perish. That's what we mean by holding up Christ as a fact of history. He is the new possibility that God has given the human race, each one of us, the possibility of life instead of death. That's what enabled Martin

Luther King to say when he accepted the Nobel Peace Prize, "I believed that unarmed truth and unconditional love will have the final word in reality." That could happen if ever the human race decided to accept Jesus Christ. We have that choice. It is a fact of history.

II We must hold up Christ not only as a fact of history but as *the Master of Life*. Someone expressed it this way: "There was once a poet by the name of Homer, and he wrote poetry. After that, people did not have to reckon how great a thing poetry might be. They saw it for themselves and read it. So also there was a philosopher once by the name of Socrates. Since then we have not had to reckon how great a thing philosophy might be. We can go and see it for ourselves. By the same token, there was a Master once of life. He spoke of it in terms of beauty, reverently. He lived out its immortal destiny with clear and lofty grandeur, carrying it unhurt through death. Men saw him do it and wrote it down. Since then, nobody has had to suppose or presume or hazard a guess that life, after all, may be a very great thing."[21]

How great a thing it is comes clearly into focus when we hold up our lives against his. I saw a symbol of that contrast when I visited the Louvre Gallery in Paris and came to a famous piece of sculpture called "The Gladiator." It is a life-sized statue of a Greek athlete poised in the act of throwing the discus. The artist, whose name can be faintly deciphered in the marble, took perfection as his model — a human figure beautiful to behold, ideally proportioned, and perfect in symmetry. It wasn't the statue that caught my attention; it was a group of shabbily-dressed French boys accompanied by a teacher. They were all blind. Deprived of sight, they had to appreciate the treasures of the Louvre through touching and hearing. The teacher took one small fellow in his arms and lifted him up so that he could touch "The Gladiator." The contrast brought tears to my eyes. Here was a thin, spindly-legged little lad reaching up to embrace this marble specimen of perfect physical manhood.

I have often thought of that as a parable. Christ is the Gladiator, the model not only of physical manhood but of **full-orbed human personality** at its highest and best. When we hold up our lives against his we feel as emaciated and deprived as the little blind boy and we understand the words of Paul which the New English Bible translates, "We are deprived of the divine splendour" (Rom. 3:23). Christ is the divine splendour, the representative man, the man par excellence, the true splendour of manhood which God created and intended for each one of us. He is the Master of life.

Because Christ is the Master of life, we can trust his teachings about life. In all other areas we consult the masters to learn the rules, techniques, and principles that have made them great. Jesus was very explicit about some of the principles that controlled his life. He said, "My food is to do the will of him that sent me, and to accomplish his work" (John 4:34 RSV) — a life controlled by perfect obedience to the will of God. He said, "Love one another as I have loved you" (John 13:34 RSV) — a life controlled by the faith that love, being final truth and ultimate reality, is the secret of right relations among men. He said, "Even the Son of Man came not to be served but to serve" (Mark 10:45 RSV) — a life controlled by the principle that we find fulfilment not by commanding people but by serving them. If we had read these teachings for the first time in some ancient manuscript, having no clue as to the teacher's identity, we might dismiss them as an impossible ideal. We trust them because Christ said them and because they were the principles that governed his own life.

These can be the principles that govern our lives. We needn't be dismayed by the contrast between his character and ours. God sent Jesus into the world not as an impossible ideal but as a visible goal toward which we can all strive. Christ wants to be the Master of our lives, he wants us to take his teaching and character as our living model, he wants us to follow and obey and imitate him so that he can help us to achieve our potential and rise to our full stature as children of God. Christ is greater than religion. That's why the purpose of evangelism is not to commend our religion but to hold up Christ in all the splendour of his manhood, so that each person may see him and say, "Lord Jesus, your life is the highest I know. I cannot call the highest I know a lie. I must call the highest I know the truth. But that means that the Eternal is like you. Behind the externalities of this strange universe is a Spirit, the truth about which we know when we see you. Therefore I commit myself to you. I promise to obey you. Take control of my life. Be my Master, my Lord."

III

We must hold up Christ not only as a fact of history, not only as the Master of life, but as *a Saviour*. We can describe a Saviour as someone who brings us help from the outside and rescues us from an impossible situation. Here is a person who has fallen into a deep pit and broken his legs in the fall. He cannot climb out to safety on a ladder of good resolutions, because the ladder must be fastened at the top. Only if someone from above comes down to him in his darkness and helps him upward to the light has he any hope of being saved. Christians believe that Christ is the hand of God reaching down and rescuing us from our impossible situations. They believe that God sees us in our human predicaments; sees that we are at the mercy of temporary ignorance, mass social forces, and our own endocrine glands; sees us caught up in a spiral of inexorable circumstance, doing what we do not want to do, making decisions that we do not want to make, and letting loose upon ourselves evil powers that betray our plans and curse our hopes. And God says, "My children have fallen into a deep pit, they are trapped, they cannot help themselves. I shall send them a Saviour to rescue them from their darkness and bring them upward to the light."

We can describe a Saviour as someone who stands between us and danger. When I was a small child, my father and I were walking in a field where we saw a cow with a calf. I tried to pet the calf, and that angered the mother cow who lowered her head and charged in my direction. My father jumped in front of me and drove her off, otherwise I might have been injured, perhaps killed. Instead, he might have been injured or killed. He interposed his body between me and danger; he was my saviour. Christians believe that when Christ died on the cross he interposed his body between us and the worst suffering that the world can inflict. He made his body a shield that breaks the force of scourge, thorns, nails, and spear. Because of him we can say with Paul, "We are afflicted in every way, but not crushed; perplexed, but not driven to despair; persecuted, but not forsaken; struck down, but not destroyed; always carrying about in the body the death of Jesus, so that the life of Jesus may also be manifested in our bodies." (2 Cor 4:8–10 RSV).

We can describe a Saviour as someone who proves himself

stronger than our enemies. He defeats our enemies and breaks their power, so that we are saved from them though we continue to fight them. When the allied forces landed on the French coast they turned the tide of the Second World War. V-Day did not come for many months, but D-Day decided the issue. The occupied countries in Europe fought with new hope because they were fighting on the winning side and because they knew that final victory was assured. It was Oscar Cullmann who first drew the parallel and reminded us that Christ's D-Day was Easter Day, when he burst the bonds of death and won the decisive battle against all the forces of evil that proved too strong for the unaided strength of men. The certainty of his final victory saves us from despair in the face of all that is evil and malignant in our own lives and the life of the world. Though the battles continue, we know that the war has been won, the long struggle between sin and grace will have an end, the kingdom of God will be revealed in its fullness, and Christ's eternal purpose will be accomplished.

We can describe a Saviour as someone who is always there when we need him. By instinct he seems to know when we are depressed or in trouble, and that's when he comes to us, writes, or telephones. He brings comfort and encouragement, carries part of the burden, adds his strength to ours. The risen Christ promised his disciples, "I am with you always, to the close of the age" (Matt. 28:20 RSV); and Christians have found this promise to be triumphantly true. To people who accept Christ as Saviour he is the most present reality in their lives, as real as parent, child, husband, wife. They speak to him, listen to him, consult him, and draw their inspiration from him. He is their strength, their purpose, their hope, their very reason for being alive. Because he lives, they live also. He is their Saviour.

Ernest Gordon, Chaplain at Princeton University, made the discovery that Christ is greater than religion in a Japanese prison camp during the Second World War. He tells about it in his distinguished book *Through the Valley of the Kwai*.[22] There came a time of spiritual awakening among those diseased and hopeless prisoners of war when they decided that they wanted to learn more about Christianity, and they asked Captain Gordon if he would lead them in a discussion group. He said that he didn't feel qualified or even very convinced. He had more or less turned away from religion at university. However, he agreed to do it, but he didn't talk to them about religion. He talked to them about Jesus. He held up Christ as a flesh and blood man whom they could understand and admire and follow, who was nailed to a cross and was not broken by it. That made sense to the men. They responded, and others will respond when we hold up Christ as a fact of history, as the Master of life, and as personal Saviour. Christ is greater than religion.

THE FIRST GREAT DUTY OF RELIGION

There is a familiar figure in the twelfth chapter of Mark's gospel. We meet him in the temple at Jerusalem on the Tuesday of Holy Week, the last week of our Lord's earthly life. That was the day when the religious leaders engaged Jesus in public debate and tried to trap him with tricky questions. Jesus proved to be more than a match for them. In fact, the wisdom of his answers befuddled their minds and made them look foolish. At last one of the scribes, sensing the Master's superiority, came forward and asked, "Which commandment is the first of all?" Sensing the man's sincerity, Jesus answered by quoting the scriptures. He said, "The first is, 'Hear, O Israel: The Lord your God, the Lord is one; and you shall love the Lord your God with all your heart, and with all your soul, and with all your mind, and with all your strength'." To that commandment he linked a second. "The second is this: 'You shall love your neighbour as yourself'." He added, "There is no commandment greater than these." When the scribe wholeheartedly agreed with him, Jesus said, "You are not far from the kingdom of God" (Mark 12:28–34 RSV).

We have all known or heard of people of whom it could be said that they were not far from the kingdom of God. They might not claim to be inside the kingdom, if that means being inside the institutional church and assenting to all its orthodox beliefs. Yet although they remain outside the community of religious faith, they display to a remarkable degree the essential spirit and character of religious faith. P.L. Jacks, the English philosopher, referred to such a person when he said, "Look at him. Isn't he an inspiration? He spends his breath arguing that there is no God, but spends his life proving that there is." The church in its evangelistic appeal ought to pay more attention to people like that, because the church has much to give them and much to learn from them. They see what we in the church often fail to see.

The scribe in the temple perceived two very important truths. To begin with, he saw that the first great duty of religion is to love God. In recent years the church has tended to lose sight of that first commandment and has put all its emphasis on the second — "Love your **neighbour as yourself.**" Some branches of the church have become almost humanistic in their disregard of God and theology and the means of grace, insisting that the only relevant form of Christianity is one that engages in political action and community service. People outside the church applaud the sense of social responsibility. At the same time, like the scribe in the temple, they can see that the first duty of religion is to love God, for in loving God we find both the motive and the inspiration to love our fellow men.

The temple scribe perceived also that love for God must involve the whole personality. The rock opera *Jesus Christ Superstar* depicted Mary Magdalene as a reformed prostitute — which makes interesting drama; though it has no biblical basis. She sings a haunting song about Jesus, "I don't know how to love him.... He's just a man .... And I've had so many men before." But Jesus was not just a man, he was God incarnate, and we do know how to love God. We are to love him with the whole of ourselves, not just part of ourselves, or else God becomes only a part of all that he can be to us. That's what Jesus meant when he said, "You shall love the Lord your God with *all* your heart, and with *all* your soul, and with *all* your mind, and with *all* your strength." The first great duty to religion is to love God, and it must be a love of the whole personality.

I We are to love God with our *minds*, which means that we are to love him reasonably and intelligently. John Wesley once received a letter from a pious person who declared, "The Lord has directed me to write you that, while you know Greek and Hebrew, he can do without your learning." Mr. Wesley replied, "Your letter received, and I may say in reply that your letter was superfluous, as I already know that the Lord could do without my learning. I wish to say that, while the Lord does not direct me to tell you, yet I feel impelled to tell you on my own responsibility that the Lord does not need your ignorance either."

That's not to say that only a scholar can love God. Many of the greatest saints were not scholars; they did not know Greek and Hebrew. One of them was a Sunday School superintendent in a little country church where I served as pastor. He had the equivalent of a Grade Three education and could barely read and write. Yet I have never known a person who loved the Lord more than he did. And it was a reasonable love. He knew what he believed, he knew his Bible, he responded to the teaching element in sermons, he could discuss the doctrines of the faith. He was so firmly rooted in the truth that it would have taken a hurricane to topple his structure of belief.

We must love God not only with the mind but with the whole personality, yet the mind is a good place to begin. More people would find religion intellectually credible if they approached and studied it with the same spirit of inquiry that they devote to other disciplines. Just to read the Bible with open minds would bring them to a deeper understanding of the faith. Michael Bourdeaux, writing about the church in Russia, tells of a young communist in the Stalin regime who was converted to Christianity by reading the gospel of Matthew. It was a purely intellectual conversion at first. He said that the New Testament, especially the teachings of Jesus, appealed to him more than the literature which he had been forced to read at university. His love for God began with the mind.[23]

The love for God does not stop there but it ought to begin there in order to lay a firm foundation for the whole structure. You hear people say that they have no time for reading theology but would rather serve God in some practical way. That's like building a house without the foundations. There was never a more practical Christian than the apostle Paul. His New Testament letters tell us all that we need to know about applied Christianity. Notice, however, that the practical thrust in any of Paul's letters invariably begins half-way through with the stout word "therefore" and follows as a consequence of the theological position which he has stated in the first part of the letter. Again and again he says, in effect, "We believe certain truths. Therefore we must act in a certain way." Theology comes first. Our love for God begins with the mind.

I heard a scholarly Jesuit say that if the Christian faith offended his reason at a single point, he would leave the church tomorrow. He may have been demanding too much of his reason. At the same time, why do many intellectual giants hang on to the Christian religion in a day when so many intellectual pygmies are abandoning it? The answer is that they have thought out their religion. They have applied to it the same mental disciplines that the scientist applies to his science and the mechanic to his machines. They love God with their minds. That's where our love of God has to begin. That is the first great duty of religion.

II We are to love God with our *souls*. The Bible sees the soul as the seat of the emotional life, implying that love for God should be an emotion that we feel deeply. That is true of any kind of love, especially married love. A young man who proposes to a girl simply because a computer has declared them compatible would be loving her only with his mind, whereas true love is an emotion that only music and poetry can express. It makes you laugh and cry; it raises your blood pressure, sets you on fire and throws your deepest feelings into turmoil.

The great saints and mystics have felt that way about God. They have loved God deeply, as a bride loves her husband, a parent his child, or a patriot his country, and they have poured out their love in the devotional legacy of the ages. Listen to the hymn writer

> Thee will I love, my strength, my tower,
> Thee will I love, my joy, my crown,
> Thee will I love with all my power,
> In all my works, and Thee alone,
> Thee will I love, till sacred fire
> Fills my whole soul with chaste desire.[24]

Some people sneer at honest emotion in religion. They dismiss as phoney any experience of God that springs from the way a person feels; they say that it's not genuine or sincere or lasting. On a television panel, following a documentary about the "Jesus Freaks," a psychiatrist gave his judgment that such religion could not possibly amount to much because it is obviously a matter of emotion. I wanted to shout back at the screen, "What's wrong with that? We display emotion in the love of family and country. Are we too decorous to be emotional toward God?"

Of course, we don't manufacture the emotion of love; it is a response to that which is loveable in the beloved. As the New Testament writer says, "We love God because he first loved us" (I John 4:19). The most dramatic example in the gospels happened at the house of a Pharisee where Jesus was a dinner guest and where a woman of the streets crashed the party (Luke 7:36-50 RSV). She knelt at Jesus' feet, washed them with her tears, wiped them with her hair, and anointed them with costly ointment. When Jesus saw that her behaviour scandalized the company he told a story about two debtors, one of whom owed a large sum of money, the other a small sum, and the creditor forgave both. Jesus asked, "Now which of them will love him more?" Then he pointed to the woman and said, "I tell you, her sins, which are many, are forgiven, for she loved much; but he who is forgiven little, loves little." Love for God is our emotional response to all that God in his love has done for us, and the more we realize what God has done, the more deeply we shall love him in return.

There was a Roman Catholic priest who announced to his congregation that he would preach about the love of God. Stepping down from the pulpit, he took a lighted candle from the altar and walked over to the great crucifix. Without saying a word he held the candle so that all could see the nail-pierced feet of the dying Saviour. Then he lifted it to the wounded side and pinioned hands. Finally he let the flame fall on the agonized face and thorn-crowned head. The great congregation sat and wept. Their emotions had been stirred, as God intended his love to stir human emotion. The cross is the innermost depths of God's suffering love laid bare before the whole world, and from the depths of our souls we must respond in love.

III We are to love God with our *hearts*. Hebrew psychology saw the heart as the seat of man's moral nature, implying that to love any person with the heart is to be committed to the best in that person. F.W. Robertson, a British preacher of the last century, tells what it means to love God with the heart.

> To love God is to love his character. For instance, God is Purity. And to be pure in thought and look, to turn away from unhallowed books and conversation, to abhor the moments in which we have not been pure, is to love God. God is Love; and to love men until private attachments have expanded into a philanthropy which embraces all — at last, even the evil and our enemies with compassion — that is to love God. God is Truth. To be true, to hate every form of falsehood, to live a brave, true, real life — that is to love God. God is Infinite; and to love the boundless, reaching on from grace to grace, adding charity to faith, and rising upwards ever to see the Ideal still above us, and to die with it unattained, aiming insatiably to be perfect even as the Father is perfect — that is to love God.

That was the constant theme of the great prophets of Israel. When they accused the people of honouring God with their lips while their hearts were far from him, they simply meant that their religion did not get beneath the surface and involve the innermost thoughts and motives and purposes of their lives. Therefore it was unacceptable to God. "What doth the Lord require of thee, but to do justly, and to love mercy, and to walk humbly with thy God" (Micah 6:8 KJV). That was a matter of spiritual logic. Only a just man can love a God who loves justice. Only a merciful man can love a God who loves mercy. Only a humble man can love a God who loves humility. We love God with our moral nature, or we do not love him at all.

"You can't believe in God and steal apples!" That angry outburst came from Luis Cortez, a young Puerto Rican who worked with boys in the East Harlem Protestant Parish in New York. Bruce Kenrick wrote about him in his book *Come Out The Wilderness*.[25] One evening some teenagers burst triumphantly into the church hall with a crate of apples which they had stolen. Luis turned on them furiously. "So!" he shouted. "You meet here in the church and you go out and raid the stores. You think you're smart. I tell you, you're fools! One day you'll do this and the cops'll come. And when they come they'll shoot. They won't care whether they plug you in the leg or in the heart." The boys stood motionless as Luis glared at them. "And listen," he said, "I'll tell you something. You can't believe in God and go and steal someone's apples. It's wrong! You just can't do it!"

There are all sorts of things that you can't do and don't want to do when you love God with your heart. You don't want to steal, cheat, lie, gossip, commit adultery, or anything that insults the character of the God who has revealed himself in the perfect character of Jesus. To love God is to love him with your whole personality. That's what Jesus told the Samaritan woman who tried to divert attention from her own immoral life by engaging him in a discussion about the right and wrong place to worship God. He said, "God is spirit, and those who worship him must worship in spirit and truth" (John 4:24 RSV), meaning that you worship God with yourself, with the kind of person you are; and if that kind is not acceptable to God, then you have to change it, you *want* to change it. That's what it means to love God with your heart.

IV We are to love God with our *strength*. That should appeal to those eager Christians who want to roll up their sleeves and get on with the business of serving God in a practical way. Jesus pointed to practical Christianity as an integral part of our total love for God, the part that proves all the rest. In the last analysis you always prove your love for a person by what you do for him. You love him with your strength.

The risen Christ made that demand of Peter on the shore of the Sea of Galilee. Three times, corresponding to Peter's three denials of him on the eve of the crucifixion, he asked, "Simon, son of John, do you love me?" Peter protested, "Lord, you know that I love you" (John 21:15vvRSV), but if he really loved his Lord he would have to prove it not only in words but in deeds, not only in feelings but in resolute and courageous action. Christ has always been asking that question of his servants. He asked Martin Luther, "Do you love me enough to break with a corrupt church and stand alone when all men stand against you?" He asked William Wilberforce, "Do you love me enough to fight the inhuman slave trade and suffer the scorn heaped upon any person who threatens a nation's economy?"

Come back to the temple in Jerusalem. After saying to the scribe, "You are not far from the kingdom of God," Jesus showed his disciples a person who was actually in the kingdom. She was a poor widow who dropped two copper coins in the collection plate — a mighty act of generosity because it was all the money she had (Mark 12:41-44). To love God with your strength means giving him that which truly represents yourself, that which costs you money, time, energy, and labour. It works out in different ways with different people. One person tithes not only his money but his time, giving one-tenth of his time to the service of God in the church and community. Another person, a medical specialist, gives two months every year, at his own expense, to treating patients and training other doctors in the developing countries. Not that they give only a fraction of themselves. Those acts of costly practical service are the overflow of complete commitment to God. They love God with their strength.

Karl Barth, the great theologian, was in Berlin after the Second World War meeting with some of the Communist leaders of East

Germany. The President said to him rather piously, "Herr Professor, what we need in Germany is the Ten Commandments." Barth replied quickly, "Yes, Herr President, especially the first."[26] Let the people in Germany or any country give their first loyalty to God, let them give him their first love, and they will see all other loyalties and loves in the right perspective. The first great duty of religion is to love God with the whole personality — "with all your heart, and with all your soul, and with all your mind, and with all your strength." When we love God with all of ourselves, we allow God to become all that he can be to us.

A GREAT PRICE FOR A GREATER TREASURE

"Again, the kingdom of heaven is like a merchant in search of fine pearls, who, on finding one pearl of great value, went and sold all that he had and bought it" (Matt. 13:45,46 RSV). That's all there is to the parable of the Pearl of Great Price. It is one of the shortest parables that Jesus ever told — not at all like the Good Samaritan or the Prodigal Son, which have a stage setting and a cast of characters and a plot with a beginning, climax, and ending. All we are given is a single statement in one sentence telling us that the kingdom of God is like a pearl merchant who all his career dreams of finding a pearl of surpassing value and when he finds it says, "I must have it — at any price." So he sells his whole collection of pearls and presumably his house and everything he has in order to buy it, because it is worth more than all of them put together. He pays a great price for a greater treasure. We must use our imagination to flesh out the details, and that presents a challenge.

One person who accepted that challenge was John Steinbeck. He wrote a short novel called *The Pearl*,[27] which is really the New Testament story in reverse. It is about pearl divers somewhere off the coast of South America, dark-skinned men who tied rocks to their bodies and went down to the bottom of the sea searching for treasure. Like the merchant in Jesus' parable they all dreamed of finding a pearl of surpassing value. Kino, the hero of the story, needed to find it desperately, because his infant son, Coyotito, had been stung by a scorpion, and the doctor refused to treat him without payment. While his wife, Juana, clutching her suffering baby, waited in the canoe, Kino searched the ocean bed. At last he came to the surface and threw some oyster shells into the bottom of the boat. They pried open the largest one, and there it lay in all its translucent beauty — the pearl of the world.

The news travelled fast, and soon the whole village was wild with excitement. Visitors clustered around the brush hut, including the priest and the doctor who pressed his services even though the baby seemed to have recovered from the scorpion bite. Kino was now a rich man. What would he do with his new-found wealth? He decided that he and Juana would have a proper wedding in the church. They would have Coyotito baptized. There would be new clothes for the child, an education. For fear of thieves Kino hid his pearl that night beneath the dirt floor of the hut. He didn't have to wait long. A scratching sound awakened him, he sprang in the darkness, a blow on the head nearly stunned him. The thief escaped. "This pearl is a sin," cried Juana. "It will destroy us. Throw it away, Kino." "No," he replied stubbornly. "Tomorrow we shall sell it. This is our only chance."

No one worked next morning, because the whole village followed Kino in a strange procession through the brush huts to the streets of the city where the pearl merchants had their offices. News of the giant pearl had reached them, and they reeled with excitement as they thought of getting their hands on it. They were very sure that it would fetch a fortune, but that's not what they told Kino. In a callous, disinterested way they told him that the pearl was too large and ugly, it had no value except as a collector's item, and they offered him a paltry sum for it. His neighbours urged him to accept; but Kino, knowing himself cheated, cried out, "My pearl is not for sale here. I will go to the capital." But what way is open to a man who defies the whole system, the whole way of life? Kino had lost one world and had not gained another. Back in his hut the thief struck again, nearly killing him this time. Again Juana cried, "Kino, this pearl is evil. Let us destroy it before it destroys us. Let us throw it back in the ocean where it belongs."

That night Kino awakened to see his wife rise from her bed and stealthily leave the hut. He followed her to the water's edge where she raised her arm as though to throw something. He caught her arm, wrenched the pearl from her hand, struck her on the face, threw her down on the rocks, and kicked her on the side, the woman he loved. Suddenly something hit him from behind. He lunged with his knife at the dark figure, and a man lay dead at his feet. In that instant Juana knew that the old life was gone forever. "You have killed a man," she cried. "They will come for us.... We must be gone before daylight." Kino stumbled toward his canoe, his means of escape, but a great hole had been knocked in the bottom. They turned back toward their brush hut to take refuge there and heard the crackling roar of the fire that consumed it. Still Kino clung to his pearl. "It has become my soul," he said. "If I give it up, I shall lose my soul."

Only the mountains offered them any safety now. At night they travelled on foot, Juana carrying the baby. By day they hid from the trackers whom they knew were following them. Higher into the mountains they climbed and, looking down, they saw the trackers, three of them, armed with rifles. At last Kino knew that he would have to kill them or be killed by them. Leaving Juana in a cave with the baby, he stalked down the craggy mountain until he came where two of the men slept and the other kept watch. Even as he sprang, the man's rifle exploded, and Kino heard a scream from the cave.

In the late afternoon Kino and Juana, carrying a limp little bundle, trudged back into the village, looking neither to the right nor to the left. When they reached the edge of the water they stopped and stared out over the Gulf. Kino looked at the great pearl in his hand. In its surface he saw the baby, Coyotito, lying in the cave with the top of his head shot away. And the pearl was ugly; it was gray, like a malignant growth. Drawing back his arm, he flung the cursed thing with all his might. He and Juana saw the little splash in the distance. They stood there watching the place for a long time.

II Those two stories, our Lord's parable and Steinbeck's novel, are both about pearls, but they are as different as day and night. The first is a story of blessing, the second a story of curse; the one a story of gain, the other a story of loss. In exchange for a precious pearl the merchant in Jesus' parable willingly sells all that he has. In exchange for a precious pearl the poor pearl diver unwillingly loses his child, his home, his means of livelihood, his friends, his freedom — nearly everything that is of any value to him. Yet apart from these differences the two stories are really like two sides of the same coin, and they teach the same message — that every good thing in life has to be purchased at the expense of a lesser good. The richest treasures always come at a very high price. Some treasures are so costly that they take all we have in exchange for them. They are the pearls of life, and nearly every person has his pearl.

It may be the pearl of human love, as it was for King Edward VIII of England. Some of us remember that handsome young man, the darling of the British Empire, who succeeded his father, George V, to the throne. We remember our sense of shock when he abdicated in less than a year, gave it all up in order to be free to marry a woman, twice divorced, whom he called "the woman I love." The whole story is told in a fascinating book by Ralph Martin called *The Woman He Loved*.[28] It seems that the King did love Mrs Simpson whom he had been seeing secretly for a long time against the advice of his family, the Prime Minister, and the Archbishop of Canterbury; they all warned him of the price that he would have to pay. At last he took her husband to lunch and said, as if he were discussing a precious art treasure, "I must have her." He got her and lost the throne. She was his pearl of great price.

There is nothing fictitious about Jesus' parable and Steinbeck's novel. That scenario is being played out on the stage of real life all the time, and it teaches us that the best things in life are not free. The best things are costly, so costly that sometimes they claim everything else that we have. It is a lesson that we try to teach our children, though how can we expect to teach them when many of us have not learned it ourselves? How shall we convince them that in this life they can't have it both ways? They can't have their own collection of pearls *and* the pearl of great price. They have to choose one or the other, and they really grow up when they learn to confront the cost of their own choices. It is a mark of maturity to know that everything has its price tag attached and that we can maintain some values only by sacrificing other values. So there is always one question to be asked: Is it worth it?

Sometimes it is not worth it. Some treasures, like Kino's pearl, are not only too costly but too all-consuming. They seem almost alive with their voracious hunger to devour everything in sight. Better to throw them away. There was a business man who reached that difficult decision in middle-age at a time when it was nearly too late. From earliest years his pearl had been wealth and success, and he gave everything in exchange for it. He rose rapidly, he succeeded, he made money, but he paid a terrific price in the sacrifice of his own happiness and the happiness of others. His wife, whom he loved but treated as an adjunct to his career, drank heavily and had to be sent to hospital. His son, whom he loved, but neglected, committed suicide. His daughter, whom he loved, left home without leaving her address. He had no close friends to whom he could turn for sympathy and help. Yes, he made money. That was his pearl, but in the end he threw it away because he realized that it was not worth the price.

When we look at the other side of the coin, we see that the opposite is true. Some of life's pearls have such surpassing value that they are worth more than we can ever pay for them, even worth the loss of everything else. That's what we try to teach our children when we encourage them to get an education. Here is a young person with the potential and the opportunity to become a doctor. To achieve that goal he must sacrifice his freedom, his independence, his earning power, and his leisure for many years. It is a difficult choice to make and to live with. One day, however, he completes his course, and a career of supreme usefulness and fulfilment opens before him. He now has a distinctive role to play in the world, and he will be happy in it. That is his pearl of great price, and he sees that it is worth more than anything it could possibly have cost him. A great price for a greater treasure.

III Jesus spoke about the kingdom of God. The parable of the Pearl is one of the stories he told which begins, "The kingdom of God (or the kingdom of heaven) is like this . . ." Sometimes he speaks of the kingdom as though it were in the future, even beyond history — a new age where all peoples and nations acknowledge God as King and give him their obedience. At other times he speaks of the kingdom as if it were already here. He says, "The kingdom of God is within you" (Luke 17:21 KJV) or "among you" — a personal relation to God which we can seek, enter, and possess here and now. Thus a courageous pastor in Germany could say to his congregation during the dark days of war, "In, with, and under the world's anger and distress, in, with, and under the hail of bombs and mass murders, God is building his Kingdom."[29] He is building it in the hearts of the people who obey him. Jesus spoke of his own coming as the kingdom of God breaking in on history. He began his public ministry by saying, "The kingdom of God is at hand" (Mark 1:15 RSV), as though to say, "It is here. I am the kingdom of God," suggesting that to be in the kingdom is to be with him and committed to his way of life. As such it is like a pearl of great price, the richest treasure that life affords, worth more than anything we can possibly pay for it.

Entering the kingdom of God in that sense might be compared to a change of citizenship. For many years peoples from other parts of the world have been emigrating to North America with little money in their pockets and no material possessions but the clothes on their backs. The reason is that they have had to leave it all behind. That was the price they paid to escape political tyranny. A husband and wife from Czechoslovakia, both medical doctors, came to Canada on a research fellowship and never went back, though it meant giving up their home and their positions. They didn't see much future for their own careers in Canada, but they chose to live under a democratic government where at least they could see a future for their children. Freedom was their pearl. They have paid a great price for it.

We pay a great price; we leave a lot behind in order to live under the government of God. Jesus said, "Anyone who wishes to be a follower of mine must leave self behind" (Mark 8:34 NEB), or as the older version translates it, "deny himself." In the kingdoms of the world we are continually being urged to do the very opposite — affirm ourselves, enjoy ourselves, indulge ourselves. That is the mood of our culture, the theme of many television commercials, the platform of every political party, the rallying-cry of the labour unions. Nobody applauds the person who stands up today and says, "Do without some of those luxuries and expensive holidays, forget your own comforts and pleasures, think of other people, work for the common good." Yet that is the price we pay to emigrate from the kingdoms of the world to the kingdom of God. What do we get in return? Jesus described the reward in the form of a paradox. He said that by denying yourself you find yourself, you become the person you really are, the person whom God created you to be. That may explain why the happiest people are usually those who leave self behind. Perhaps they are too busy doing the will of God to think of themselves and therefore of the things that could make them unhappy. They pay a great price.

We must leave behind our neutrality if we want to enter the kingdom of God, because there is no room for neutrality in the kingdom. "He who is not with me is against me," said Jesus (Matt. 12:30 RSV). To be in the kingdom is to be with Jesus in the sense of being committed to him and involved in the work that he is doing in the world. That is a costly choice to make, because it means that we may have to give up apathy for adventure, comfort for character, desire for duty, happiness for hard work, security for self-fulfilment.

It means also, however, that we shall become a part of the most supremely creative, transforming force that the world has ever known. We shall shape history. When Jesus walked this earth, there were two realities in the world — a dying empire that looked to the past, and a newborn religion that looked to the future. There are two realities in our world — a sick civilization that seems to be dying, and a company of the committed that contains the seeds of new life. To that company belong the men and women of our generation who take their stand with Jesus. They pay a great price.

We must leave behind our lesser loyalties when we enter the kingdom of God. Jesus said, "No one can serve two masters" (Matt. 6:24 RSV), and he specified mammon (money) as a master — which it is in many people's lives. They don't control their money; it controls them. They worship money like a god, they trust and serve it and give it their first loyalty. That was the "rich young ruler's" problem, and that's why Jesus told him to give his money away (Mark 10:17-22). Of course, that admirable young man wanted eternal life, and you can't ask for much more than that. He wanted the quality of life which he saw in Jesus, life which is so vitally and vibrantly alive that it goes on forever, even beyond the experience that we call death. Only God gives eternal life, because only God himself is eternal. To enter the kingdom of God is to share the eternal life of God. But God alone is King in his kingdom. There can be no other kings, no other lords and masters. Lesser loyalties must go. That is a great price to pay, but it is a great price for a greater treasure.

IV To the Apostle Paul the pearl of great price was Christ himself. For the sake of Christ this gifted young man gave up his ancestral ties, his racial identity, his vocation as a Jewish rabbi, his promising career, his material security, his place of prestige in the community. Writing to the Philippians he lists all the things that he lost for the sake of Christ, quickly adding that they were of no more value than garbage compared to what he gained. Read his words.

> Whatever gain I had, I counted as loss for the sake of Christ. Indeed I count everything as loss because of the surpassing worth of knowing Christ Jesus my Lord. For his sake I have suffered the

loss of all things, and count them as refuse, in order that I may gain Christ.... that I may know him and the power of his resurrection, and may share his sufferings, becoming like him in his death, that if possible I may attain the resurrection from the dead. (Phil. 3:7-11 RSV)

There you have our Lord's parable put into practice and applied to a human life. There you have a man who was, in fact, like a merchant in search of fine pearls and who, on finding the kingdom of God, which was like a pearl of great price, went and sold all that he had and bought it. For Paul Christ *is* the kingdom of God. Christ in his own person shows us the perfect relationship between God as King and man as subject. He obeyed God's will even when it meant death on a cross. He lost everything in his obedience to God, and God gave it all back when he raised him to glory. If we share the obedience, says Paul, we shall share the glory, and *that* will be our pearl of great price.

WHAT IS TRUE GREATNESS?

The American author, Edwin Newman, has written a humorous book about words called *Strictly Speaking*.[30] He says that in any American political convention the word most frequently heard is "great." Everything is great, everybody is greater, and America is always the greatest. He recalls a Democratic national chairman who introduced the keynote speaker by saying that he had great pleasure and privilege, plus great pleasure and personal pride, in presenting a great American who was a great, able, and outstanding member of a great deliberative body. Even the clergymen who pray at the beginning and end of each session are great. All of which leads to one of two conclusions: (1) There must be a lot of great people about, or (2) the word "great" has lost its value, like the dollar on world markets, and should be taken out of circulation until it recovers its true meaning and worth.

We have been looking at the way that Jesus used the word "great." He used it so rarely that on his lips the word really means something, it has value. He applied it to himself only once when he said, "I tell you, something greater than the temple is here." Twice he used it to praise the quality of a person's faith, "I have not found so great a faith, no, not in Israel." He said that the commandments to love God and one's neighbour are great commandments. He compared the kingdom of heaven to a pearl of great price. On one occasion, possibly two, he told his disciples who the great people really are and gave them a definition of true greatness.

I It is always fun and sometimes funny to play the game of deciding who are the great people, especially if we are tempted to nominate ourselves for the honour. Even the most humble folk have been caught playing that game. One day Jesus caught his disciples arguing among themselves as to which of them was the greatest. That surprises us. We expect to hear such arguments among athletes, actors, politicians, and even preachers, but not among disciples of Christ. Jesus silenced that argument by pointing to a child and saying, "Whoever humbles himself like this little child, he is the greatest in the kingdom of heaven" (Matt. 8:4 RSV), but his disciples didn't understand.

This is obvious from another incident which happened later on. Jesus, followed by the disciples, was on his last journey to Jerusalem where he expected to ascend a cross and establish a spiritual kingdom. Three times he told them what was going to happen, but again they did not comprehend. They expected him to ascend a throne and inaugurate a political kingdom; and if Jesus were about to be crowned king, they wanted to be in at the beginning when he began appointing his chief ministers of state. Suddenly James and John sent their mother up to Jesus with an outlandish request, "Command that these two sons of mine may sit, one at your right hand and one at your left in your kingdom" (Matt. 20:17ff RSV).

Now follows a private dialogue between Jesus and the two ambitious disciples (apparently their mother was not drawn into it). The dialogue reveals at once the honesty of Jesus and the loyalty, or perhaps the ignorance, of the disciples. "You do not know what you are asking," said Jesus. "Are you able to drink the cup that I am about to drink?" That could only be the cup of suffering and death which he had just predicted, the cup that he would ask God to remove in the eleventh hour — "My Father, if it be possible, let this cup pass from me" (Matt. 26:39 RSV). With fine honesty he asked his disciples if they could share that cup with him. With commendable loyalty they said, "We are able." If sharing Christ's glory meant sharing his suffering, they were willing to face that suffering. And they did face it eventually, as Jesus foretold — "You will drink my cup," to which he added, "but to sit at my right hand and at my left is not mine to grant, but it is for those for whom it has been prepared by my Father."

That seems to be the end of the private dialogue. The other ten disciples seem not to have overheard it. They did overhear the mother's request, however, and they reacted to it immediately. Like animals at feeding time they milled around their Master, all scrambling for preferment and babbling indignantly against these two opportunists who had tried to get ahead of them. They also were ambitious men, and if an honours list was being drawn up, they wanted their names to rank high on it. After all, they had been among the party faithful from the very beginning, and if the party were now to assume political power, they wanted their rightful share of political plums. They couldn't possibly have overheard the private dialogue, because they were thinking of discipleship not in terms of suffering but in terms of personal greatness.

Jesus dealt with them very patiently. He did not explode at their obtuseness or blaze at their blindness. Gently and lovingly he told them that greatness in the kingdom of God is not the same as greatness in the kingdoms of the world. "You know," he said, "that the rulers of the Gentiles lord it over them, and their great men exercise authority over them." In the kingdoms of that world the standard of greatness was power. A person was counted great according to the number of people he controlled or the measure of service he could command. The very word "great" conjured up an image of the Roman governor with his retinue, the Eastern potentate with his slaves, the wealthy merchant with his servants, the proud priest with his acolytes. The world saw greatness as a pyramid. The higher one climbed, the fewer his equals and the more his subordinates; and if one were the greatest of all, he might sit in solitary, commanding majesty on the pyramid's peak.

That is still the world's standard of greatness. When we ask, Who are the great people? we think of those who "lord it over" the rest of us, those who have power to command and control. We think of the military "top brass" who only bark an order and whole divisions of officers and men spring to attention and salute. We think of the politicians who can change our way of life, and of bureaucrats who advise the politicians. We think of industrialists who can throw thousands out of work, bosses who can put us through sheer hell, union leaders who can strike a country into chaos, journalists who mould public opinion like putty.

These are the "great" men as the world defines greatness; and if we are honest we shall admit that we are sorry not to be included in their distinguished company. We wanted it for ourselves once, and now we want it for our children. The proud parent who scans his son's report card with approval and says to himself, "Some day my boy will be a great man!" sees his offspring at the peak of the pyramid where he can look down in lordly power and command many people to serve him. Such is the world's standard of greatness.

That is not Christ's standard, because he turned it upside down. To the ambitious request of the disciples, all twelve of them, he said what must have exploded like a bomb in their minds — "It shall not be so among you, but whoever would be great among you must be your servant, and whoever would be first among you must be your slave." In the ancient world no person ranked lower than the slave who served the guests at a banquet; yet Jesus said that the slave is the great person in the banquet of God's kingdom. He said that greatness in God's order of life does not consist in commanding others to do things for us; it consists in what we willingly do for others. He said that God honours us not for the service we receive but for the service we give — and the greater the service, the greater the honour. Jesus inverted the pyramid, so that the peak is no longer at the top but at the bottom. That means that the closer a person gets to the peak, the lower his prestige, the heavier his burden, and the more people he carries in love.

II That is not an unworldly ideal but one which the world unconsciously accepts. The world will respect and sometimes fear the people of power, but the world admires, loves and remembers the people who serve it — the politician who sees himself as the servant of his constituents, the scientist who spends himself unsparingly for humanity, the physician who will come out at any hour of the day or night to heal a patient, the merchant who cares for his customers, the teacher who really cares for her pupils. This is no rule for saints and heroes alone but a rule of practical common sense, validated by life itself.

To support that truth we might take an opinion poll and begin by asking — Who is the greatest man of the twentieth century? *Time* magazine answered that question a few years ago by nominating the late Dr Albert Schweitzer. His motive to serve came into focus when he was twenty-one years of age and very conscious of the advantages that life had given him and of his obligation to share those advantages. By that time he had already distinguished himself as a scholar and musician, but in his heart he knew that if he really wanted to follow Jesus he must serve his fellow men in some active and practical way. Therefore he resolved that until his thirtieth year he would live in the service of knowledge and art, and after that give himself utterly to serving people where they needed him most.

That is what Schweitzer did. At age thirty he gave up those other careers for a time, returned to university and qualified as a doctor of medicine. His friends tried to dissuade him against going to Africa as a missionary, but he said, "For me the whole essence of religion is at stake.... The meaning of my life does not consist in knowledge or art but simply in being human and doing some little thing in the spirit of Jesus." For fifty years this brilliant man spent himself utterly in the most incredibly primitive conditions continuing the healing ministry of Christ. Many people never did probe the motives behind his amazing career of self-renunciation and service, but they respected and admired it, and they knew that it was a force stronger and more lasting than all the tyrannies, machines, and nuclear weapons of our modern age. Albert Schweitzer showed the world that the path of greatness still lies in the way of lowliness and unselfish service. He proved the saying of Jesus, "Whoever would be great among you must be your servant."

If we took another poll and asked, Who is the greatest living person in the world today? we might be surprised how many people would nominate a Roman Catholic missionary nun named Mother Theresa who lives and works in India. She was awarded the 1978 Balzan Prize for humanitarianism, peace, and brotherhood among nations, and the 1979 Nobel Prize for peace. After teaching for twenty years at the Loreta Convent School in Calcutta, Mother Theresa realized quite suddenly that outside the pleasant, cloistered atmosphere was a world of misery where her real work lay. Given permission to leave the convent, she immediately went to the most wretched part of the city, found lodging, gathered together a few abandoned children, and started her ministry of love. In 1949 she founded her new order, The Missionaries of Charity.

The order has grown at a fantastic rate. Today there are houses in twenty-five Indian cities and in several other countries. The sisters, in addition to the usual vows of poverty, chastity and obedience, take a special vow to give wholehearted service to the poorest of the poor, whose life they totally share. They provide a home for little children unwanted by their parents and for infants who might otherwise be thrown away or killed. They have nearly 10,000 lepers under their care, and with new drugs they are often able to cure that dread disease. They have picked up 23,000 dying people from the streets of Calcutta and taken them to their Homes for the Dying, where they show them that they are wanted and loved even for the few hours that they have to live. Mother Theresa admits that what they are doing is only a drop in the ocean, but she believes that the ocean would be less without that missing drop. Malcolm Muggeridge wrote a book called *Something Beautiful for God*[31] in which he says concerning this remarkable woman, "It will be for posterity to decide whether she is a saint. I can only say of her that in a dark time she is a burning and shining light; in a cruel time, a living embodiment of Christ's Gospel of love; in a godless time, the Word dwelling among us, full of grace and truth."

III A former missionary in West Africa tells how he taught true service to an intelligent boy, the nephew of a paramount chief. He had arranged a meal for some of his church members and he asked this boy, along with others, to serve at the table. The lad flatly refused. He said that he would serve the missionary in any personal capacity, however lowly, but he would not serve these people. "Do you realize," he said, "that these people's ancestors were slaves to my uncle's ancestors? And you ask me to serve them!" The missionary showed no displeasure. He simply asked the boy to bring his New Testament and read aloud the thirteenth chapter of John's gospel which tells how Jesus, the Lord and Master, washed the feet of his disciples. The boy did so and was visibly moved. Tears trickled down his cheeks. When he had recovered his self-control he said, "If Jesus, who was the Son of God, could do that, then I, although I am the nephew of a chief, will serve these people." Years later, as a leader in his own developing nation, he wrote to the missionary, "I shall never forget the day you taught me how to serve."

It wasn't just any person who said, "Whoever would be great among you must be your servant." It was the greatest person of all. After telling the disciples that true greatness resides in humble service, Jesus pointed to himself and said, "For the Son of Man came not to be served but to serve, and give his life as a ransom for many."

The apostle Paul in his Letter to the Philippians (2:5-11 RSV) marks the descent of Jesus Christ on the inverted pyramid of service. "He was in the form of God," writes Paul — eternally, essentially, and unchangeably God, possessed of all the divine majesty and power. Yet "he did not count equality with God a thing to be grasped," did not hug his Godhead jealously but laid it down willingly for the sake of men. "He emptied himself" — gave up the glory of divinity to take upon himself our humanity. He took "the form of a servant" — the lowest form of humanity, that of a slave to God and his fellow men. He humbled himself as a slave and "became obedient unto death, even death on a cross" — a criminal's death — so that he might meet us at the deepest point of our sin and lift us up to God. In sacrificial service and love resides the greatness and glory of Christ. It is a new kind of greatness, a new kind of glory.

What was God's verdict on the humility of his obedient Son? God's verdict was to turn the inverted pyramid right-side-up, so that the peak was now at the top. "Therefore God has highly exalted him," writes Paul, "and bestowed on him the name which is above every name, that at the name of Jesus every knee should bow, in heaven and on earth and under the earth, and every tongue confess that Jesus Christ is Lord, to the glory of God the Father." To his obedient servant Son, God gave a greater glory than the world could ever give — the adoring worship of the whole universe. It is a figure of what God has in store for us if we can heed the words with which Paul begins this tremendous passage: "Have this mind among yourselves which you have in Christ Jesus." The person who has the mind of Christ does not want to be counted great in the kingdoms of the world; he wants only to be counted great in the kingdom of God. And he knows that one question alone will decide his greatness — How many people has he served? "Whoever would be great among you must be your servant."

The Greatest is Forever

WORDS THAT NEVER PASS AWAY

Looking over the garden fence, my next-door neighbour found me in a gloomy mood. "What's wrong?" he asked. "That's what's wrong!" I grunted, kicking the lawn sprinkler. "It won't work any more, and I've had it only two years." It was one of those plastic affairs manufactured cheaply and, of course, it couldn't be repaired. We agreed that they don't make lawn sprinklers like they used to. We agreed that they don't make cars or houses or anything else like they used to. Time was when those things were built to last. We were protesting against the throw-away syndrome that Alvin Toffler wrote about in his book, *Future Shock*.[32] He showed that one of the by-products of rapid social change is transcience, which means that nothing lasts, nothing is intended to last. Manufactured goods have a built-in obsolescence. You don't repair the broken lawn sprinkler; you throw it away and replace it. So with the disposable razor and the ballpoint pen and numerous other items which are almost symbolic in their fragility.

The throw-away syndrome is not new. Nothing man creates is built to last forever — manufactured goods, cars, houses, institutions, governments, nations, civilizations. Even God's creations do not last forever. Jesus said that heaven and earth will pass away, and that is true even apart from the cataclysmic act of God which he predicted. The throw-away syndrome gives new urgency to one of our basic human needs. Now as never before we are asking, "Does anything last? Is anything permanent? Is there anything in the ocean of change to which we can anchor our lives?" Jesus gives the answer. In a passage that prophesies the end of the age he says, "Heaven and earth will pass away, but my words will never pass away" (Mark 13:31 RSV). He refers to the words of that particular prophecy, but history shows that he spoke the truth in a larger sense. The words of Jesus, the teaching he gave, the promises he made, the word of God that was in him, survive all change. These never become obsolete. They have a profound and timeless relevance to life in every age. They are the greatest, and the greatest is forever.

I   There are three reasons why we can trust the immense claim of Jesus concerning his own words. We believe that they will never pass away because they are *rooted in God*. In a throw-away society we are looking for something that we don't have to throw away because it lasts, it is permanent, it endures. In an age of changing ideas and values we are looking for eternal truths that never change. Such truths have to be rooted in God, because only God is eternal. That's what makes him God. Before the mountains were brought forth, or ever he formed the earth and the world, even from everlasting to everlasting he is God (Ps. 90:2).

Some people don't like to be told that heaven and earth will pass away. There was a lady who cried out in horror when an astronomer said that the world would probably come to an end in a billion years. He tried to reassure her by saying, "But not before a billion years." She sighed with relief and exclaimed, "Thank goodness! I thought you said a million." A billion or a million — the world will come to an end because it had a beginning. It is not eternal. Only God and the words that are rooted in God are eternal. We can trust those words and hang on to them and believe that they will endure even when heaven and earth pass away.

We trust the teachings of Jesus, because they are rooted in God. He specifically said, "The words that I say to you I do not speak on my own authority; but the Father who dwells in me does his works" (John 14:10 RSV). It requires a mighty exercise of faith to believe that immense claim; but when we do believe it, even death appears in a different light. There was a time when death darkened the home of Thomas Carlyle. A sympathetic friend tried to comfort him by quoting the familiar words of Jesus, "In my Father's house are many mansions" (John 14:21 KJV). "Aye," muttered the bereaved man, "if you were God you had a right to say that; but if you were only a man, what do you know any more than the rest of us?" The point is that Jesus *did* know more than the rest of us, he knew more about God because God was in him. His words about life and death were rooted in God and are therefore true, everlastingly true.

How vitally important today that we hang on to the words of Jesus about man's dignity as a child of God! Because he called God his Father and the Father of each one of us, we know that he believed, as no one before or since has ever believed, in the all-surpassing worth of persons. That belief shines in everything he says and does. It looks out of his eyes when they are happiest and when they are saddest. It trembles in his most loving consolations and thunders in his most passionate rebukes. It is the inspiration at once of his pity and his indignation. Daringly he taught that even the loftiest institutions and regulations of religion must take second place to the interests of persons, for they are the servants and not the masters of the human soul, and so by implication are democracy and culture and science, and all other systems and organizations that have their little day and cease to be. Systems vanish, but persons are eternal in the love of God. That's what Jesus taught.

How important in this age of rapid change that we hang on to his teaching about the future course of history! It was a teaching full of hope, and that's not the same as optimism. The mood of optimism can give way to despair, as it did in the case of an idealist who grew up in the early part of this century. After the two world wars he wrote, "A whole lifetime's optimism was disintegrating."[33] Optimism does disintegrate because it is essentially a faith in man, in man's ability to resolve his predicaments and work out his problems. It jauntily asserts that everything will turn out all right when, in fact, everything may not turn out all right. Hope, on the other hand, is a confidence in God — in his love, his purpose, his power, his control of human life and history. It says in the words of Jesus, "Fear not, little flock, for it is your Father's good pleasure to give you the kingdom" (Luke 12:32 RSV). Those are words we can trust, words that will never pass away, because they are rooted in God.

II Another reason we believe that the words of Jesus will never pass away is that they were *incarnate in Jesus himself*. Even if his lips had never spoken them, his life would still have proclaimed them. Words themselves are not eternal; personality is eternal. "Ideas," wrote George Eliot, "are often poor ghosts. Our sun-filled eyes cannot discern them. But sometimes they are made flesh, they breathe upon us with warm breath, they are clothed in a living human soul. Then their presence is a power." The words of Jesus have lasting power because they were clothed in his flesh, breathed with his breath, and lived out by him as a workable way of life on the stage of history. Behind all his words stands his own life, incarnating and illustrating everything he said.

Listen to one of his words about happiness. He was speaking to a woman in the crowd, probably a mother herself, who had just called out, in effect, "Your mother must be proud of you. You must make her very happy." Jesus replied, "No, happy are those who hear the word of God and keep it" (Luke 11:28 NEB). He might well speak about happiness, for he was a supremely happy person, the happiest in Palestine, who raised people's spirits and brought cheer to troubled hearts wherever he went. The secret of his happiness was his obedience to the will of God. He had heard the word of God and kept it. What else could account for his deep and quiet joy as he confronted the cross, a joy so abundant that he shared it with his sorrowing disciples: "These things I have spoken to you, that my joy may be in you, and that your joy may be full" (John 15:11 RSV).

Jesus shared another secret when he spoke about the paradox of gain and loss: "Whoever seeks to save his life will lose it; and whoever loses his life will save it, and live" (Luke 17:33 NEB). People do lose life when they try to save it. There was a man who retired from business at age fifty and devoted himself to golf, gardening and afternoon tea. He refused to do anything strenuous or really useful, saying, "One must keep fit." He died at age fifty-five during an operation for a complaint which proved to be non-existent. The surgeon said he died of fright. Jesus says that the way to save life is to lose it, spend it, give it away, and his own life demonstrated that truth. He gave away his time, energies, sympathies, material possessions, and went on giving until it took him to the last full measure of devotion on a cross. Jesus lost his life and found it eternally.

Jesus spoke many words about prayer; and we can trust what he said, because he himself prayed as naturally as he breathed. In every crisis, before every decision, and even with his dying breath he spoke to God in prayer. His ministry moved back and forth like a pendulum between God and the world, every encounter with men was followed by an encounter with God, and every period spent with God was followed by involvement in the affairs of men. Prayer was the habit of his life, and it made such a difference to him that the disciples, who themselves were men of prayer, begged him to teach them how to pray. That's when he gave them and us the model of all praying — "Our Father, who art in heaven, Hallowed be thy name . . ." (Luke 11:1vv KJV). We can hang on to that pattern prayer, not only because it teaches us how to pray, but because it is the prayer of the Teacher.

Sir William Osler, the great teacher of medicine, used to say that he accomplished more in fifteen minutes at the bedside than he did during two hours in the classroom. He meant that his students learned by being with him, watching him work and listening to his words as a commentary on his work. That is even more true of the words of Jesus. To realize their truth we must be with him, and look at his life and listen to his words as a commentary on his life. Then we shall trust his words, we shall cling to them, and we shall know that they will never pass away because he will never pass away. He is "the same yesterday, today, and forever" (Heb. 13:8).

III We believe that the words of Jesus will never pass away because they have been *validated in human experience*. In this age of change and transience and novelty, when so many people suffer the stress of "future shock," the church is not like a doctor prescribing another new remedy and saying to a patient, "Try it for a while. It won't do you any harm, and it may do you a lot of good." The words of Jesus are a very old remedy which people have been taking for the past two thousand years, a remedy which has healed them and saved them because it has proved valid in human experience.

That is one respect in which the words of Jesus differ from the plays of Shakespeare or the Dialogues of Plato. We have the greatest respect for those works of literary art and wisdom, but we would not quote them to a dying person or a crowd of refugees. We might quote the words of Jesus which have proved valid in *every* human experience and which speak to us at every stage of life — sickness and health, weakness and strength, sadness and happiness. Even when heaven and earth pass away in our own lives, when our little world comes to an end and we lose all its securities, we can still turn to the words of Jesus and in them find courage and strength to endure.

There was a stalwart minister of the gospel who made that discovery about all that Jesus said concerning the love of God. At age forty he was struck by polio and, though by sheer will power and God's help he defied all medical predictions and returned to his pulpit within a year, it was with a body badly handicapped. Then his eldest son, an outstanding lad who intended to offer himself for the ministry, enlisted in the army and was blown to bits by an enemy shell. My friend carried on with courage but again suffered illness — a stroke that partly paralyzed him and for a time robbed him of coherent speech. Meanwhile his devoted wife, who for years had been suffering from Parkinson's disease, became steadily worse, and after a last desperate attempt to save her life by brain surgery, she slipped quietly away. Soon afterwards my friend went to join his wife, having drunk the cup of sorrow and suffering to its bitterest dregs. Yet the fire of his faith burned brightly to the very end. In his last days he radiated a strength and serenity that seemed to come from the other world. Asked the secret, he said, "I have found God in a new and wonderful way. For years I have believed and preached what Jesus said about the love of God. Now I know it to be true."

Countless people have borne a similar witness to the moral teachings of Jesus which have proved valid in human experience and have stood firm against the criticism of every generation since the days of his flesh. Even today, when every sphere of thought and action continually undergoes revolutionary change, the wisest people offer no amendment to or deletion of the Galilean program of life. They realize that the words of Jesus are more than a "wisdom literature" designed to regulate the conduct of a certain type of living in a given epoch. They are timeless and universal and are as applicable to the modern, mechanized occidental as they were to the ancient oriental ploughing his overworked soil with a crooked stick.

They have been prescribed as a remedy for the human spirit suffering the tension and stress of a throw-away society. Some of us were on a pilgrimage to the Holy Land. When we came to a mountain beside the Sea of Galilee, a psychiatrist in our party conducted a service of worship based on the Beatitudes (Matt. 5:1vv). He said that most mental disorders arise out of wrong relationships, and shared his conviction that the Beatitudes, enunciated on that very mountain, contain the highest wisdom ever given for achieving right relationships. He went through those words of Jesus one by one, showing us that meekness, mercy, purity, and the rest are the practical expressions of a right relationship of love which alone brings complete health of personality. "This is still a new teaching," he said. "Most of my patients have not heard of it or, if they have heard of it, they have never seriously put it to work in their lives. But it does work. It proves valid in human experience."

"Heaven and earth will pass away, but my words will never pass away." I thought of that verse at the New York World's Fair where a torpedo-shaped capsule was sunk three hundred feet in the ground, presumably to be discovered five thousand years from now. It contained a variety of objects which will enable people in the year 6965 to document our civilization as it was in the year 1965. One tries to imagine their reaction. They may wonder, for example, what we did with a tiny scrap of cloth known as a bikini and how our eardrums stood the rhythms of a record made by the Beatles. A transistor radio, a plastic heart valve, and a computer memory unit will show them that we made marvellous progress, but tranquillizer pills and filter cigarets may indicate that we were not too progressive. Most of the objects in the capsule will seem dated and totally strange to them, and they may wonder if we possessed anything of enduring value. Then they will find a Bible which, we dare to believe, will be as familiar to them as it is to us and as it was to our ancestors. In it they will read the words of Jesus, words rooted in God, incarnated in Jesus himself and validated in human experience, and they will rejoice as we rejoice in the truth of what he said: "Heaven and earth will pass away, but my words will never pass away."

THE LOVE THAT NEVER SEPARATES

An old man lay dying in the public ward of a city hospital. His life had been a struggle against grinding poverty and crippling ill-health. There seemed nothing for him to live for, and death would have been a happy release. A hospital chaplain, of the old school, wanting to know if the patient belonged to any church, stopped by his bed and asked him, "What persuasion are you, my friend?" "Paul's persuasion," came the quiet reply. That puzzled the minister. He knew about Catholics and Protestants and Baptists and Presbyterians and the rest, but "Paul's persuasion" had him frankly mystified; so he asked, "What do you mean, my friend?" With difficulty the old man half raised his head from the pillow and said in soft, yet vibrant tones, *"I am persuaded that neither death, nor life, nor angels, nor principalities, nor powers, nor things present, nor things to come, nor height, nor depth, nor any other creature, shall be able to separate us from the love of God, which is in Christ Jesus our Lord."*

The quotation comes from the eighth chapter of Paul's letter to the Romans (vv38,39 KJV). Every person ought to be "persuaded" of something. Especially in these days of changing values every person should have at least one thing of which he can be sure, one great, eternal, unchanging, and dependable reality to which he can cling, even if his whole world goes to pieces. For Paul and for the old man in hospital that reality was the love of God. They believed not only that God loves us but that he never stops loving us, that nothing can make him stop loving us, and that nothing can come between us and God's love.

"I am persuaded," writes Paul. There is something to be said for that sturdy old translation in the King James Version, as compared to the Revised Standard Version which reads, "I am sure," and the New English Bible that puts it, "I am convinced." It usually takes some kind of outside pressure to "persuade" a person. It may be the pressure of physical force such as dictators use when they try to persuade a victim to sign a confession. It may be the pressure of verbal argument that batters a man's mental resistance until it breaks down and he cries out, "All right, you can stop. I am persuaded!" It may be the pressure of undeniable facts.

Facts persuaded Paul to believe in the inseparable love of God. He may not always have believed it. He may have refused to believe it in theory, even fought against it; but God had demonstrated his love, made it real, visible, and actual on the stage of history and brought it so redemptively into Paul's experience that he could never again doubt its reality. Paul had seen the fact of God's love in Jesus Christ, a love so high that it reaches to heaven, so deep that it reaches to hell, so wide that it circles the stars, so long that it spans eternity. From *that* love of God, the limitless love revealed in Jesus Christ, Paul was persuaded that nothing can ever separate us.

Paul is persuaded, but has he persuaded us? He tries to do so, not with bullying dogmatism, but with the earnest manner of a man who wants to share the richest treasure that he has ever discovered. He knows that *we* may not be certain of God's love in Christ, we may not be sure that God loves us, we may be thinking of all sorts of things that can separate us from his love. So Paul tries to help us. Sensing the unspoken arguments of our minds, he conjures up all the terrors that assault the soul, all the enemies of faith and assurance, all the forces that destroy confidence, and he challenges them to do their worst.

I   The first one is *Death*. "I am persuaded that neither death, nor life . . ." Paul begins with death, because in our human relationships it is the Great Separator. The grim reality of death is that it does separate us from those whom we love, and nothing can soften the sorrow of separation. No peaceful parting, no precious memories, no words of comfort and assurance can ease the pain of a bereaved husband who leaves the cemetery with a broken heart, having committed to the earth all that is mortal of the woman whom he has loved for a lifetime. The all-consuming fact in that man's experience is that when he gets home, his wife will not be there to greet him. Death has separated her from him. But not from his love. Though he does not see her, he will not cease to love her. He will go on loving her as dearly and tenderly as he did through all the years of their marriage. He will go on hoping that she still loves him, still belongs to him, still waits for him in eternity.

If we have the hope that death does not fracture our love for each other, can we believe that our dying fractures God's love for us? Not if we have seen God's love made visible and actual in Jesus. Long before Jesus lived and died on this earth, there were people so sure of God's love that they believed that death could not separate them from it. The Hebrew shepherd who wrote the twenty-third Psalm, when he remembered how God had brought him into the world, watched over him and provided for his needs, met him at every turn of the way and never failed him, could not imagine that the loving, caring God would desert him at death. The God who had played a part in his every experience would surely play a part in the greatest experience of all. "Surely goodness and mercy shall follow me all the days of my life: and I will dwell in the house of the Lord forever" (v.6 KJV).

The God of the twenty-third Psalm is the God who "so loved the world, that he gave his only begotten Son, that whosoever believeth in him should not perish, but have everlasting life" (John 3:16 KJV). He is also the God who raised his Son from the dead. That means that God's love is stronger than death. It means that the person whom God loves still has to die, but death will not be the end of his life with God; it will be the transition to a new stage of his life with God. Let this belief be sufficient. One reason people have trouble with the Christian faith is that they get lost in its derivative beliefs, and lose sight of the great essentials. It isn't essential to know what happens to us after we die. Such knowledge may be as much beyond our grasp as poetry is beyond the grasp of an animal. It is enough to know that God loves us and to have faith that death cannot separate us from his love.

Such was the faith of a Christian pastor in Japan who, before his untimely death, wrote a message to his congregation. He said that when his daughter told him that the doctors had diagnosed his case as inoperable cancer, he felt as if a black cloud were pressing down on his chest, and he was resisting it with all his strength. He tried to pray but could only keep crying like a child, "My Father, my Father in heaven..." Yet that was enough. Simply to be in the presence of the God who loved him as a father, simply to know that approaching death could not separate him from the Father's love, took away his fear. He wrote, "I went to sleep and slept restfully. And when I awoke, an amazing strength had been instilled into my heart. Since that time I have not experienced the sense of fear again."

II   Paul passes now from the lesser to the greater peril: "I am persuaded that neither death, *nor life*...;" and there is no doubt that it is more difficult to live with faith than to die with faith, if we live in touch with reality. Imagine someone who has known nothing but pain and hardship, imagine a man whose family is hungry and poorly housed because he cannot find work, or imagine a woman whose husband is a drunkard and a brute, saying, "I am persuaded that this life of fear and misery cannot separate us from the love of God!" If we read the eighth chapter of Romans without knowing who wrote it we should suspect that the author, whoever he was, must have led a singularly secure and sheltered life to allow for a faith so joyous and triumphant.

Secure? Sheltered? Someone else, perhaps, but not the apostle Paul. Read his other letters, especially Second Corinthians where he frankly tells of all he has suffered for the sake of the gospel (11:24vv). Paul knew what it was to have friends turn traitor, to be beaten with rods, to be stoned, shipwrecked, imprisoned, maligned, and slandered, to be treated as a renegade and a turncoat. He knew what it was to fight with wild beasts, to battle against ill-health, to lose all his money in a lawsuit with the civil authorities. Those things loomed so large in his experience that he deliberately threw them in the face of the Corinthian church. He might have said, "I am persuaded that life is full of ugly and distressing things! I am convinced that life is a nightmare between two nothings!" Paul knew that all the ugly things are there. He knew that the world is full of wasting and destroying forces. He knew also, however, that the love of God is eternal and more powerful than any of them, and he hung on to the faith that nothing in life could separate him from that love.

It is one of the harsh realities of life these days that people are so easily separated from each other's love. Not only material things but human love has become a casualty of the throw-away society. Even marriage joins the list of disposables. Toffler predicts that it will soon be quite normal for the average person to have two or three careers and two or three marriages during his lifetime. When they reach a certain stage in life, after living together for ten or twenty years, a couple will decide that it's time for a change and will amicably shake hands and go their separate ways. They will announce, "We have decided to separate," as calmly and casually as they would announce, "We have decided to sell the house."³⁴

People are not like houses, however; and divorce, to call it by its right name, is rarely calm, casual, and amicable. More often it is emotional, traumatic, and shattering. As someone has said, "It is an unnatural smashing of that which was built to last . . . an amputation inflicted on a living body." It leaves broken hearts and hurt lives. To be rejected by the one person who has always accepted you, to be separated from the one love of which you were always sure, can be a devastating experience from which some people never recover. In their sorrow of heart they can only turn to God who never rejects them and to his love which is the only love of which they can be eternally sure.

So it happened to George Matheson, one of Scotland's ablest preachers and one of the world's great writers of devotional literature. His familiar hymn, "O Love that wilt not let me go," has brought comfort and healing to countless human hearts. He wrote it on the eve of his sister's wedding, a difficult occasion for him because it reawakened his own mental suffering. He once loved a woman whom he wanted to make his wife, but he had to tell her that he was going blind. She loved him but not enough to share his handicapped life. His blindness separated him from her love. In his brokenness and despair of soul he turned to the love of God in Jesus Christ, a love from which nothing in life can ever separate us. He wrote the beloved hymn under a moment of inspiration, saying, "I had the impression of having it dictated to me by some inward voice rather than of working it out myself."

> O Love that wilt not let me go,
>   I rest my weary soul in thee;
> I give thee back the life I owe,
> That in thine ocean depths its flow
> May richer, fuller be.
>
> O Joy that seekest me through pain,
>   I cannot close my heart to thee;
> I trace the rainbow through the rain,
> And feel the promise is not vain
> That morn shall tearless be.

> O cross that liftest up my head,
>   I dare not ask to fly from thee;
> I lay in dust life's glory dead,
> And from the ground there blossoms red
> Life that shall endless be.

III Paul now projects on the screen of our minds a long procession of all the enemies of faith and assurance, declaring that not one of them can separate us from God's love in Christ. We can go even further and put Paul's "persuasion" to the acid test. Suppose we simply *refuse to be loved by God?* Suppose we throw up a barrier of indifference, pride, and unbelief, declaring rebelliously, "We have no God!" — does that not separate us from his love?

If that's what we believe, it only shows how lamentably we underestimate the toughness, the stubbornness of God's love in Christ. We think of it as a passive affection waiting to be reciprocated; whereas it is active, persistent, dynamic, pursuing us to the uttermost limits of our rebellious pride. "Whither shall I go from thy Spirit? Whither shall I flee from thy presence?" cried the writer of Psalm 139, a man whose great discovery about God is that we cannot get away from him. "If I ascend up into heaven, thou art there: if I make my bed in hell, behold thou art there. If I take the wings of the morning, and dwell in the uttermost parts of the sea; Even there shall thy hand lead me, and thy right hand shall hold me . . ." (vv7-10 KJV). The God of the psalmist is the God who "so loved the world, that he gave his only begotten son," the God whose Son prayed on a cross for his crucifiers, "Father, forgive them; for they know not what they do" (Luke 23:34 KJV). That's what persuaded Paul as no theological argument could ever have done. Pushing his way through the maze of life to a cross, he heard God saying, "You can do with me what you like. You can break my bones and bruise my flesh and drain my blood, but you cannot stop me from being what I am — the Father who loves you and will not let you go."

Graham Greene's novel, *The Heart of the Matter*,[35] portrays an English chief of police in an African colony, a man whose bitter frustration has involved him in a tangled web of intrigue, adultery, and murder. Beside himself with despair, he lunges toward the brink of suicide. Religion has ceased to guide and comfort him, but in a gesture of defiance he goes to the church for the last time, more to curse God than to pray. As he stands before the altar and looks at the crucifix, there breaks upon him, as never before, the amazing awareness of One who clings to him in spite of all that he is and all that he has done. The indignity of it almost disgusts him, and he cries out, "How desperately God must love me!"

God does love us desperately, he loves us defiantly; and the cross is the great act of defiance — God thrusting himself into the midst of our sinful situation, acknowledging us even when we do not acknowledge him, accepting responsibility for us and standing by us even in our shame. We sin against God, but God will not be compromised by our sin. We break our friendship with God, but God will not let that friendship be broken. We contradict God, but God, in turn, contradicts our contradiction. We defy God, but God answers with a superior act of defiance. The heavenly Father loves us so desperately, so defiantly, that he will not stop loving us even though we refuse to be loved by him. No barrier of indifference, pride or unbelief, nothing in our intellect, our emotions, or our conduct, nothing we can think or say or do can separate us from God's love made visible and actual in the cross of Jesus Christ.

"For I am persuaded that neither death, nor life, nor angels, nor principalities, nor powers, nor things present, nor things to come, nor height, nor depth, nor any other creature, shall be able to separate us from the love of God which is in Christ Jesus our Lord." That was Paul's persuasion, and it can be our persuasion — the one thing of which we are sure in this age of changing values, the one great, eternal, unchanging, and dependable reality to which we can cling even if our whole world goes to pieces. We can believe it, trust it, and stake our lives on the truth of it. In its power we shall rise above every possible condition of existence, every unseen influence or force, every uncertainty of time, every extreme of space, every conceivable thing in this world and in the world to come.

THE FRIEND WHO NEVER FAILS

The attractive teen-age girl was convulsed with tears. That's how she reacted to the news that her father, a successful business executive, had just been promoted and transferred to another city — for the second time in three years. Soon the family would have to pull up roots and join him there. They would move to a bigger house in a more expensive neighbourhood and all have more money to spend, but that offered small comfort to the poor girl who could only think of the friends whom she had to leave behind. Friends are important to a girl in her mid-teens. Who would take their place? Would she stay long enough to be accepted and make new friends in the new school and community?

Another casualty of the throw-away society is friendship. That's because the whole pattern of life in a changing, mobile, transient society offers little opportunity for the kind of commitment that leads to lasting friendships. It has been estimated that in some major American cities the average residence in one place is less than four years, and it is well known that some apartment dwellers are almost as nomadic as Arabs in the desert. One doesn't make friends in those brief stop-overs; one simply settles for a few short-term acquaintances. Nor are people on the move the only ones who have difficulty making friends these days. The truth is that we relate more easily to cars and motor boats, gadgets and television screens than we do to people. We are so busy with material things that we don't have much time for people, but there is no way we can cultivate friendships without devoting time to them.

In a famous essay Ralph Waldo Emerson describes friendship as something delicate and sacred, not to be desecrated by unworthy blundering or haste. Friendship, he tells us, must develop naturally and unhurriedly, like a precious flower coming to full bloom. Emerson places the highest premium on friendship. He says, "No advantages, no powers, no gold or force can be any match for a friend." He says that friendship must be approached with the complete absence of selfishness. We must never treat a friend as property or cherish him for what he has rather than for what he is. Writes Emerson, "He who offers himself as a candidate for friendship comes up like an Olympian to the great games where the firstborn of the world are competitors. He proposes himself for a contest where Time, Want and Danger are in the lists; and he alone is victor who has truth enough and tenderness enough in his constitution to preserve the delicacy of his constitution from the wear and tear of all of these."

Emerson has described a true friend, but where shall we find one, especially in these days when human relationships have become as transient as fashions in men's and women's clothes? If we do find him, how shall we keep him in this mobile society, when we are continually commuting from one place to another? Jesus Christ offers himself as such a friend. He says to us, as he said to his disciples, "I am with you always." Christianity at its heart is not a religion or a way of life, a creed or an institution but friendship with a person, Jesus Christ. He offers himself as the Saviour of our souls and the Lord of our lives, but first he offers himself as a friend. He is the friend who never fails us and whom we never have to leave behind. He goes where we go, he meets us when we arrive. He says, "I am with you always, to the close of the age" (Matt. 28:20 RSV).

I The words, "I am with you," may be understood in two ways. They may be taken to mean, *"I am beside you, among you, sharing your life."* Certainly the New Testament makes that claim for Christ. It says that, although he was in heaven with God before the foundation of the world, he came to be with us for a season and entered all the way into our human experience. He became like us and clothed himself in our flesh — all that nature of man in which he could grow, learn, struggle, be tempted, suffer, and die. He was with us in our humanity.

We see a human parallel in the experience of John Howard Griffin, an American novelist and expert on race issues who thought that he understood the problems of the black man. One day it came to him that no white person can really understand unless he can somehow step out of his white skin and become a black himself. Griffin decided to do exactly that; he shaved off his hair and underwent a series of medical treatments that temporarily changed the colour of his skin and made him look like a bald, middle-aged Negro. In his book, *Black Like Me*, written twenty years ago, he described his reaction when he looked at himself in a mirror: "The transformation was total and shocking. I had expected to see myself disguised but this was something else. I was imprisoned in the flesh of an utter stranger.... All traces of John Griffin were wiped out of existence.... The man I had been, the self I knew, was hidden in the flesh of another."[36] In his new identity Griffin crossed the colour line and for six weeks lived and moved in a hostile country that he never knew existed, a country of poverty, hate, fear, and hopelessness where the simplest things like finding a toilet and a place to eat became an agonizing problem to him. He began to think and feel like a black person, accepting his inferiority, despising his own blackness, and crying out in silent protest to the whites, "Why do you hate me so?"

That is a limited parallel, but nonetheless a parallel, to the sense in which Christ was with us. He left the security of heaven and crossed the line into our country of poverty, hate, hopelessness, and fear. He didn't simply disguise himself in our flesh; he hid and imprisoned himself in our flesh with all its limitations, perils, and suffering. He became our friend not from a distance, not simply by sympathizing with us, but by entering and sharing our life and living alongside us. He has been where we are. He knows everything about us, knows what it is to be human, knows and understands and cares. He is "with us," as he said. That's what the New Testament claims for him.

The claim that he makes for himself, however, is infinitely more immense. When he appeared to his disciples in the upper room after his resurrection he sent their spirits soaring with the breath-taking promise, "I am with you always." We cannot begin to imagine what that promise meant to them as they struggled against the fear of losing him forever. He had called them friends and had given them the most loyal, unselfish, uplifting, sacrificial friendship that any human being is able to confer on others. Then he was taken from them, and his death plunged them into grief and loneliness. Now they had him back again — but for how long? As though sensing the unspoken questions of their hearts, he gave to them and to us a promise beyond all expectation: "I am with you always, to the close of the age" (Matt. 28:20 KJV).

Christ has kept his promise. Indeed, what comes as promise from the gospels appears as fact in the Acts of the Apostles. Though they could not see his physical form, the followers of Christ felt his living presence at all times and in all places. He was their unfailing friend who came to them when they needed him most and who was just as real as he had been in the days of his flesh. If you had stopped one of them as he walked along a Jerusalem street and asked, "Where is your Lord?" he would have replied, "He is everywhere, in Judea, in Galilee, wherever we go. He is here now." Ask that question of any Christian, and he will give the same answer. At the heart of every Christian life there is a vital friendship with the living Christ. To people who believe and trust and follow him he comes as an unfailing friend, meeting them in every human experience because he has been in every human experience. Wherever we go he goes; he is there before we arrive. Henry Van Dyke wrote a beautiful hymn in which the living Christ says,

> Where the many toil together, there am I among my own;
> Where the tired workman sleepeth, there am I with him alone;
> I, the Peace that passeth knowledge, dwell amid the daily strife;
> I, the Bread of heaven, am broken in the sacrament of life.

Christians receive bread and wine as symbols of the real presence of Christ in the sacrament of life. They received them as their first meal on the surface of the moon. Astronaut "Buzz" Aldrin took with him a small silver chalice and a piece of consecrated bread from the Communion Table at his church in Houston. After they had landed, and before Neil Armstrong left the vehicle and took his first giant step, the two astronauts opened little plastic packages containing bread and wine. Aldrin read the words of Jesus, "I am the vine, you are the branches" (John 15:5). Then they joined each other and all Christians in a sacramental meal, expressing their faith that the friendship of Christ reaches even beyond the world to the limits of outer space, recalling the older translation, "I am with you always, even unto the end of the world." (KJV).

II The words, I am with you, can be taken to mean, *I am for you, on your side."* In that sense they are a great act of commitment, the very commitment which is at the heart of true friendship and which has become so rare in our mobile society. We are always being asked to commit ourselves to Christ, but here is Christ committing himself to us. The Holy Communion symbolizes that mutual commitment. The very word "sacrament" comes from the Latin "sacramentum" which means the soldier's oath of loyalty to his general and emperor. As loyal soldiers of Jesus Christ we renew our loyalty to him at the Holy Table. Christ on his side binds himself to us and pledges himself to be our unfailing friend.

What that really means can be seen as we complete the parallel in the experience of John Howard Griffin. The experiment having ended, he re-crossed the colour line into the white man's country where all doors were open to him and he was accepted again. But not for long. The reactions to his book, *Black Like Me*, were swift and vicious. Former friends and neighbours said terrible things about him and to him, they hung his effigy in Main Street and burned a cross on the hill above his house. In fact, they so threatened and terrified him that he and his family had to leave their home and community and look for a new life elsewhere. Remember, that was more than twenty years ago. John Griffin had done more than become a black physically — which could be reversed. He had become a black morally — which could not be reversed. He had identified himself with the black people, thrown in his lot with them, taken their side, and said, in effect, "I am with you always." For doing that he had to carry a cross.

Jesus had to carry a cross for the same reason. He was with people in the sense of being *for them*, with them as no other person had ever been. They came to him with their hunger and sickness of body and mind, and they felt the outgoing compassion of his great loving heart. They brought their children to him, and he blessed them and said how precious they were in his sight. Sinners came to him, knowing that he accepted them, even though he judged their sin. Jesus got into trouble because he stood up for people, identified himself with them, took their side. He protested against every dehumanizing force in business, politics, and even religion. That's why he was crucified. The cross of Jesus Christ is the everlasting pledge that he is with us always, to the close of the age.

That promise speaks directly to the church in its task because it follows our Lord's commission to his disciples, "Go therefore and make disciples of all nations, baptizing them in the name of the Father and of the Son and of the Holy Spirit, teaching them to observe all that I have commanded you" (Matt. 28:19,20 RSV). Although a long way from being fulfilled, obedience to that commission has made Christianity the world religion that it is today. When the General Assembly of the Church of Scotland in 1794 considered a resolution *not* to initiate overseas missions, the saintly Doctor Erskine of Linlathen rose to his feet and called to the Moderator, "Give me that Bible." He opened it and read aloud the Great Commission — make disciples of all nations, baptize them as Christians, teach them to follow the Christian way of life. "Those are your marching orders!" he thundered. Such marching orders! They surely seemed absurd to the eleven disciples who must have felt like a platoon of soldiers charged with the impossible task of winning a world war. But it was not an impossible task then, and it is not impossible now because Christ brought it within the reach of possibility by promising, "I am with you always. I am on your side. You don't have to fight alone. You fight with me. And God has given me the victory."

Christ has proved himself the unfailing friend not only of the church in its task but of every Christian who believes in him, trusts him, and tries to follow him. At the very least that means we are accepted by Christ, and that is the essence of true friendship. Someone wrote,

> The quickest way to kill a friendship is to poison it with good advice . . . . If your friend has disturbing shortcomings (and who hasn't) keep your mouth shut and love him, faults and all. He must have some good qualities or you wouldn't have had him for a friend. Magnify these. Don't try to 'improve' him. None of us are perfect — thank goodness. What a dull world this would be if everybody was! So be grateful to your friend for his small part in keeping the world from being dull. A friend with faults is better than no friend at all. It isn't likely that you will ever find one without any. And if you did, probably he wouldn't have anything to do with you.

Christ has a great deal to do with us and perhaps he does 'improve' us a little, or perhaps we cannot remain the same once we have known his uplifting friendship. Yet his friendship does not depend on our moral improvement. We don't have to qualify for it. He loves us in spite of all our faults and failures. He is on our side, he accepts us — no matter what.

He is the friend who says, "I am with you always, even when all others forsake." There aren't many friends like that. Some ships cannot stand up under the worst crises — bereavement, cancer, divorce, unemployment, loss of status. Fair-weather friends have a way of vanishing when you are in trouble, and they can't cope with your trouble; they have a way of reappearing when your trouble has passed. Jesus never vanishes. He is the unfailing friend who is never closer and more supportive than when we feel alone and forsaken. So it happened to John G. Paton, the great missionary to the New Hebrides, whose young wife died after only three months in those islands. He had to dig her grave with his own hands, surrounded by savage and hostile faces. Afterwards he said, "If it had not been for Christ and the friendship that he vouchsafed to me, I should have gone mad and died beside that lonely grave."

Of course, there are two sides to a friendship. Every person knows from experience that he cannot force another person to be his friend. Christ is very gracious. He does not thrust his friendship upon us. He wants to be our friend, but we have to respond by accepting his friendship. We have to be willing to be his friends. We have to take him at his word that he will be to us all that he was to his disciples — the unfailing friend who is with us always, wherever we go, and who is on our side no matter what. Then perhaps we shall express our great joy in the words of a beloved hymn:

> I've found a Friend; O such a Friend!
>   So kind, and true, and tender,
> So wise a Counsellor and Guide,
>   So mighty a Defender.
> From him who loves me now so well
>   What power my soul can sever?
> Shall life, or death, or earth, or hell?
> No: I am his for ever.

A RULE THAT NEVER CHANGES

An American representative in Paris wrote to George Washington concerning King Louis XIV, "In ordinary times he might have been a good king, but he has inherited a revolution." The same could be said about many people in secular society today. In ordinary times — say fifty years ago — they might have been morally exemplary, but they have inherited a revolution in moral standards. Not that people are intentionally bad in their conduct and outlook — just that they are not sure any more of the rules of the game. Those rules have been changing constantly since the Second World War, and some have been thrown out altogether. A modern Rip Van Winkle, who awakened after sleeping through the past two decades, would be shocked out of his pyjamas by the permissiveness of life today. He would soon discover that rules of behaviour are another casualty of the throw-away society.

The situation is not helped by religious teachers who insist that Jesus gave no rules. That heresy was proposed by a British periodical, *The New Christian*, which stated (Oct 19, 1967), "The significance of the ministry of Jesus is to be seen in his unwillingness to provide his followers with a body of doctrine or code of ethics." That is a strange interpretation of the ministry of Jesus and is simply not true. What shall we call the Sermon on the Mount but the ethical code of the kingdom of God? We do call one of its teachings The Golden Rule, though it is not pure gold in its human standard of reference, doing to others as we wish that they would do to us (Matt. 7:12). The pure gold is the admonition to love even our enemies, not because we want them to love us, but because God loves them and because we are all children of the Father in heaven (Matt. 5:44,45).

The ethic of a generous, outgoing, forgiving divine love is another of the everlastings which the church offers in this age of changing values and shifting moral standards. It is a rule of life that never changes. It is the supreme rule, the queen of the virtues without which all other virtues have no moral worth. So Paul praised it in the thirteenth chapter of his first letter to the Corinthians which begins, "Though I speak with the tongues of men and of angels, and have not charity (love), I am become as sounding brass, or a tinkling cymbal" (v.1 KJV). He went on to describe this eternal love-ethic not as an emotion that can be turned on and off like a tap but as a practical principle of caring and serving and living unselfishly with other people. It involves not so much our feelings towards others as what we do for them, not for our sake but for their sake and God's. Such love, says Paul, "never ends" (v.8 RSV). It is one of the abiding realities that survives all change.

I "*Love never ends*" is one of three translations of that verse and bears directly on the theme, "the Greatest is Forever." Also it is the commonest translation and the most accurate when set in its Bible context.

We have been so accustomed to hearing I Corinthians 13 *out* of its context that we forget that originally it was part of a letter written by Paul to correct a troublesome situation in a local church. That church was torn apart by rivalry and jealousy over what appeared to be an unfair distribution of spiritual gifts. Some of the members considered their gifts of tongues, prophecy, knowledge, or philanthropy superior to the gifts of others, and they became quite snobbish in their sense of superiority. Tactfully Paul reminds them that all means of service to the church have the same value because all derive from the same Spirit. He reminds them that without the supreme gift of love the purely functional gifts cannot serve the purpose for which they were given. Without love they lose their moral worth and do not build up the church.

Paul reminds his readers also that, apart from love, even life's noblest values come to an end, and in the closing verses (8–12) he names some of them. Prophecy is conditioned by time and circumstance, but when time comes to an end, we shall no longer need to prophesy abut God because we shall know the truth about him. Tongues, as the early Christians practised that dramatic gift, have largely disappeared except from the fringe of a few churches. Theology, the knowledge of God, changes from one generation to another, just as the knowledge of a child disappears into the knowledge of a mature man. It is like looking through coloured glass. Here and now we discern only the vague outline of spiritual realities; hereafter we shall know even as we are known, and we shall see God as directly as he sees us.

Against those fleeting values Paul sets certain everlastings, a trilogy of values that abide even when time flows into eternity. One of them is *faith*, which means reliance upon the grace of God in Christ. When we see him in whom we have believed, our faith will not be outgrown but deepened. Another lasting reality is *hope*, which means the certainty that God will complete what he has begun in Christ, a certainty that will be confirmed when we worship God in his own nearer presence. Those gifts reside in man, however; and as man must bow down before God, so faith and hope must bow down before *love*, because God himself is love. As love is eternal in God, so love is immortal in man. We may lose all else in life, but love is never lost, it never ends. "So faith, hope, love abide, those three; but the greatest of these is love" (v.13).

Paul has articulated our theme. He has said that love is the greatest, and the greatest is forever. Most of us realize the truth of that as we grow older. We realize that our permanent possessions are not the money we have made or the houses we have built or the success we have achieved but the people whom we have loved and who have loved us. All else disappears, but love never disappears, and life never disappears as long as there is love. The widow of Charles Kingsley caught that truth when she erected over her husband's grave a white marble cross bearing the inscription, "We have loved. We love. We shall love," and beneath it the words, "God is love."

There is a beautiful children's story that teaches a lesson about the unending quality of love. An Eastern king could not decide which of his two sons, Habib or Hassan, should inherit the throne, so on the advice of his wise men he gave each a sum of money and said that whoever used his money to perform the most enduring deed would become king after him. Hassan built a magnificent palace that brought admirers from all over the world and made him famous. Habib could think of nothing to equal that achievement, so he travelled many miles across the desert to consult a prophet. The old man advised him to withdraw from the contest and use the money to help his people. Before returning home, let him build an oasis in the desert where travellers could break their exhausting journey and find rest and refreshment. The day came when the two sons stood before their father. The king praised Hassan for his magnificent palace, then turned to Habib and said, "Long after your brother's palace has crumbled into the dust, weary travellers will stop at your oasis and find shade under the palm trees, still drink from the cooling springs, still give thanks for the person who built it. You shall be king because you have performed a deed of love, and love never ends."

That is the answer to people who have inherited a revolution in moral standards and don't know which rules to follow in these changing times. We can tell them that there is at least one rule that never changes, a rule that never ends. Henry Drummond wrote about it in his famous sermon on I Corinthians 13, "The Greatest Thing in the World." He said, "What is certain is that love must last. Covet, therefore, that everlasting gift, that one thing which is going to stand, that one coinage which will be current in the universe when all other coinages of all the nations shall be useless and unhonoured. You will give yourselves to many things. Give yourselves first to love."

II "Love never ends" has been changed by a modern scholar to read, *"Love never quits."* He was the late Clarence Jordan who prepared an earthy and racy translation in the idiom of the American South called, *The Cotton Patch Version of Paul's Epistles*.[37] Here is how he translates Paul's definition of love:

> Love is long-suffering and kind. Love is not envious, nor does it strut and brag. It does not act up, nor try to change things for itself. It pitches no tantrums, keeps no books on insults or injuries, sees no fun in wickedness, but rejoices when truth prevails. Love is all-embracing, all-trusting, all-hoping, all-enduring. Love never quits." (vv.4-7).

Love never quits, never gives up, never stops loving — *there* is a rule of life which is a far cry from the sentimental love that was being promoted a few years ago as a panacea for all the world's problems and as a substitute for real religion. We remember the hippies who waved placards telling us to "Make Love, not War" and who showed us by their lifestyle that they had no clue as to the gut meaning of this most loaded of all Christian words. Then came the new moralists who said that even adultery was not morally wrong if it seemed the loving thing to do in a situation. They were followed by the preachers who twisted the phrase "God is love" to "Love is God" and made that precious word as idolatrous as it was obscene. The word "love" became as devalued as the dollar on world markets, and we wondered if it ought not to be withdrawn from circulation until people could speak it with reverence again and restore its proper value.

There is no question about the proper value of the word *love* in I Corinthians 13. Paul defines love not as an easy emotion of affability but as a difficult, demanding, radical rule of life that touches every phase of human relations. Think how many marriages would be transformed if each partner loved the other with a love which is patient, kind, humble, courteous, unselfish, generous, and forgiving! Any couple contemplating marriage or divorce could well afford to read I Corinthians 13 together and pray about it every day before reaching a final decision. They might well ponder what it means that "love is all-embracing, all-trusting, all-hoping, all-enduring." They might well ponder what it means that "love never quits."

What it does mean is seen in a story written for a magazine[38] a few years ago by Bob Considine, a noted author and columnist. It is the true story of Edith Taylor who had lived happily with her husband, Karl, in Waltham, Massachusetts, for twenty-three years. Then the government sent him on business to Okinawa. After a long interval, in which his letters become less and less frequent, he wrote to tell his wife that he had secured a divorce in Mexico in order to be free to marry his Japanese servant-girl, Aiko. Edith was shattered, but she refused to accept the divorce as final. She loved Karl and could not quit loving him. Believing that what he had done must have been a matter of honour, she wrote to him begging him to send her the occasional letter. In that way she learned of the two daughters born to Karl and Aiko. Then came the dreadful news that Karl was dying of lung cancer. He feared not so much for himself as for the little girls and what might happen to them. If only he could have afforded to send them to America! At once Edith knew that her last gift to Karl must be peace of mind for these final weeks. Let him send the children to her; she would give them a home and be a mother to them. After Karl's death the girls came, but it was not easy for Edith, being a wage-earner. It meant hiring a housekeeper which she could ill afford. One day as she lay sick in hospital, wondering what would happen to the children as she grew older, an agonized decision was born in her mind. She must send for the girls' real mother and bring her to America too. When the plane bringing Aiko Taylor landed at New York's International Airport, Edith had a moment of fear; but the fear turned to compassion when she saw the Japanese girl, for she was little more than a girl, so thin and frightened, clutching the handrail. Edith embraced her; and as she took her husband's wife into her arms she asked God, "Help me to love her as if she were a part of Karl come home. I prayed for him to come back. Now he has — in his two little daughters and in this gentle girl whom he loved. Help me, God, to know that."

Concluding his story, the author asked, "Could you have loved that much?" No human being could love as that woman loved unless she were possessed by the Spirit of God. Only God loves without being loved in return, only God loves those who hurt him and reject his love and trample it in the dust as a thing to be scorned. Only the love of God never quits. The good news of the gospel is that God offers to give us his love. We cannot achieve it but we can receive it, and we can pray for it as a gift of God's Holy Spirit.

III Perhaps we are most familiar with the older translation of Paul's words, "Charity never faileth" (KJV) or *"Love never fails."* That is an optimistic and even daring translation, suggesting that while arguments, bribery, threats, and force may fail in human relationships, love never fails. It works every time; it is the key that unlocks the shut-up life, the warm sun that melts the frozen heart, the unfailing solvent of all our personal and social problems.

Sometimes life bears out that truth. General Booth of the Salvation Army tried to help a sullen man who had become a hardened criminal. The police could not get through to him. Prison and punishment only made him harder than ever. One day, after General Booth had worked patiently with him for months, the man's outward shell cracked. "Love and kindness," he sobbed as he broke down before the General's persistent love. Sometimes life bears out the truth that love never fails.

Sometimes it does not. Try telling a woman, other than Edith Taylor, who has been a devoted wife and whose husband has deserted her, that love never fails. Try telling parents, who have given themselves unsparingly to their children and who have been forsaken and insulted and shamed by their children, that love never fails. Try telling a missionary, who has spent his whole life in the services of people abroad and has seen those people kill his fellow-missionaries in cold blood, that love never fails.

Let's face it. In terms of our immediate, limited, human goals love as a rule of life fails again and again. Yet is that a reason to stop loving? What shall we put in place of love? And if love doesn't work in human relations, what does work? A powerful editorial in *The Christian Century* asked that question a few years ago when race riots were tearing the United States apart. It spoke of people who doubt the healing and reconciling power of love, perhaps because it has never been shown to them.

> Now and then petulant young Negro ministers — who have not suffered a fraction of the physical burden and personal humiliation their grandparents knew — say, 'Don't give me that love stuff. I've heard about love since I was a child. What's it ever done for me and my people?' We know, as most people do, that love can be used as a sop, a subterfuge, a facade. We know that what most men call love is about as far from what Christ and the Apostle meant by the term as you can get. Yet we insist with Christ that love is the commandment and with the Apostle that it never fails. Men fail love; love does not fail men. Men fail men; love does not fail love. The white man fails the Negro. A society structured and dominated by whites fails the Negro. The white-controlled government fails the Negro. But love — the love exemplified by Christ and hailed by the Apostle — does not fail. Abolish the word and substitute another and better one if you can; denounce the profanations of the concept, the duplicities that subvert love to evil uses; insist as you should that love includes justice as one of its essential factors. But do not deride and spurn love. Ultimately that is all we have to stand on, to work with, to hope in. Everything else fails; love does not fail.[39]

That's the risk we have to take if we commit ourselves to love as a rule of life. In these changing times, when many of life's values are passing like stars out of the sky, the church offers a rule of life that never changes because it never ends, never quits, never fails. That rule was made visible in Jesus whose name can be substituted for every mention of the word "love" in I Corinthians 13. We can say, "Though I speak with the tongues of men and of angels, and have not Jesus . . ." We can say, "Jesus is patient; Jesus is kind and envies no one . . ." We can say, "Jesus never fails . . ." In committing ourselves to Jesus we are committing ourselves to his way of love and we are taking a risk that it will not fail.

Yet is it such a risk? Not if God was in Jesus and not if God raised Jesus from the dead. The cross and resurrection of Christ are history's supreme proof of the failure of hatred and evil to defeat the power of love. Love cannot fail. It is every other way that fails. Love is the greatest, and the greatest is forever.

LIFE THAT NEVER ENDS

If people today are looking to the church with new interest and hope, it's because they believe that the church has something to offer them that they cannot find in the secular structures. They are tired of skepticism, cynicism and materialism. They have discovered that the satisfactions of the world do not satisfy them or fill their lives or meet their deepest needs. They feel shaken by the changing, transient, throw-away character of society, and they are searching for something permanent and lasting to which they can anchor their lives. They have been told that the church can offer it to them.

They have been told the truth, because Jesus makes that offer again and again, and he makes it now. He told people that the faith and the way of life which he brought to them were not only the best and the greatest but that they would last forever. He said that heaven and earth would pass away, but his words would never pass away. He promised to be our unfailing friend to the close of the age. He actually offered and still offers a quality of life that never ends. He made that offer on several occasions, none more dramatic than when he described himself as "the bread of life" and said, "I am the living bread which came down from heaven; if anyone eats of this bread, he will live for ever" (John 6:51 RSV).

Who can be indifferent to that enormous claim which speaks to one of our basic human hopes — the hope of immortality? Christians are not the only people who cherish that hope. If it were announced today that there is a spring of water high in the Rocky Mountains, and that whoever drinks of it will live forever, the airlines would be deluged with reservations to the nearest airstrip. The truth is that we rebel against our own immortality, we don't really want to die — as seen by the pathetic eagerness with which we welcome every advance in medicine and surgery that promises to postpone our death for a few years. The ultimate tragedy of our life, even when we grow very old, is that it comes to an end. Deep in the human heart is the longing for a life that never ends. We cannot be indifferent to the offer that Jesus makes: "I am the living bread which came down from heaven; if anyone eats of this bread, he will live for ever."

I To understand the truth of that claim we must notice three things about it. First, *Jesus made it in contrast to our essential* *human situation*. In John's gospel it follows the account of the Feeding of the Five Thousand, a miracle recorded in all four gospels with remarkably few variations in detail. All agree that with five loaves and two fishes Jesus on at least one occasion provided a meal that satisfied the physical hunger of several thousand people.

John's gospel takes us a step further and shows how the people reacted to this miracle. At first they were tremendously impressed — after all, it was not every day that someone multiplied a boy's picnic lunch into a banquet. There must be something special about a person who could do such a thing. Then they thought about it for a while and ceased to be impressed because they remembered that it had happened before. Moses in the Sinai Desert had prayed to God and brought down manna from heaven which satisfied the hunger not of 5,000 but of 500,000 people, and he had done it not once but over a long period of time. So when Jesus began talking about his power to provide some kind of spiritual food, the Jews reminded him that there was really nothing unique about the feeding miracle and they said, in effect, "You will have to do better than that."

Jesus was not upset or even surprised by this negative reaction. He welcomed it as an opportunity to make his own eternal claims in contrast to our transient human situation. He agreed that the feeding miracle was not so wonderful; but neither, he suggested, was the miracle that Moses performed in the desert. To be sure, God gave the wandering Israelites manna to eat, but it didn't last forever, and *they* didn't last forever. "Your fathers ate manna in the wilderness," he said, "and they died" (v.49). That was their essential situation. They died, and even a lifetime supply of manna could not have prevented them from dying.

That is the essential situation of every human being. He needs food in order to stay alive, but all the food in the world will not prevent him from dying eventually. In the past few minutes thousands of babies have been born all over the world, some into affluence, most of them into poverty. There is a wide difference between the immediate situation of a child born in a city hospital and one born in an African mud hut, but in their essential situation there is no difference. A hundred years from now the same verdict will be pronounced on both their lives, the same stark obituary — "they died."

From the legends of India comes the story of a young prince named

Siddharta Gautama who awakened to his essential situation. At his birth a prophet predicted that he would forsake his father's palace and become a wandering monk. Angered by this prophecy, the king banished every trace of religion from the palace and, to ensure that his royal son developed no morbid interest in religious matters, he shielded him from all pain and grief. Surrounded only by riches and pleasure, Gautama grew to manhood totally unaware of life's tragedies. One day, however, his chariot driver took a wrong turning, and for the first time the spoiled youth found himself beyond the shelter of the palace grounds. They passed a leper, disfigured and starving. "What was that?" asked the startled prince. "A man who has leprosy," came the reply. "Could I ever become like that?" "Yes, your highness, if you were to contract leprosy you would be just like that." Further along the road they passed an aged man, bent over, almost blind, hobbling along with the help of a stick. "Will I become like that?" asked the prince. "Yes, your highness," replied the charioteer, "as the years go by you will become like that." The chariot rushed on until finally it passed a corpse lying in a ditch at the side of the road. Again the inevitable question, and again the inevitable answer, "Yes, your highness, some day we all become like that." Later that evening, when the prince returned to the palace, he looked with new eyes on the golden pleasures that had made up his life. Where in all this material wealth was the answer to the misery and tragedy he had discovered that day? Before morning Siddharta Gautama had renounced the throne and left the royal palace to become a wandering monk in search of some better foundation on which to build his life. Today we know him by another name. We call him the Buddha.

He mirrors our essential situation. He shows us that our deepest need is a hunger that no material food, no affluence, no benefits provided by a welfare state can satisfy. It is a hunger for something that lasts, something permanent and enduring, a spiritual food that sustains us and keeps us alive through illness and old age and even through the inevitable process of dying. Christ offers to satisfy that hunger when he says, "I am the living bread which came down from heaven; if anyone eats of this bread, he will live for ever." In contrast to our essential situation and in a world where everything comes to an end, Christ offers us a life that never ends.

II The next thing to notice about this amazing offer is that *Jesus himself made it.* If some ordinary person described himself as the living bread that came down from heaven and said, "If anyone eats of this bread, he will live for ever," we should question his sanity. But Jesus was no ordinary person. He claimed to stand in a unique relationship with God. Throughout this chapter in John's gospel he continually calls God his Father and himself God's Son who came from heaven to make known the Father's love, to do the Father's will, and to nourish people with the Father's eternal life. Those claims are either absurd or true, and if they are true, what else can we do but trust them?

Even if Jesus had not made his offer in words, his life would still have proclaimed it. After the death of Charles Williams, C.S. Lewis wrote, "No event has so corroborated my faith in the next world as Williams did by dying. When the idea of death and the idea of Williams thus met in my mind, it was the idea of death that was changed." Sometimes a human personality seems too vitally alive to die. That's what attracted people to Jesus. He not only spoke of eternal life, he possessed eternal life. He seemed so vibrantly alive that they felt dead by contrast and they pleaded with him to share his secret. The Rich Young Ruler "ran up" to Jesus and knelt before him and asked, "Good teacher, what must I do to inherit eternal life?" (Mark 10:17 RSV). The hostile lawyer asked the same question, "Teacher, what shall I do to inherit eternal life?" (Luke 10:25 RSV). Even the dying thief on Calvary, having watched Jesus die, knew that the cross would not be the end of him and that soon he would be with God in his kingdom. Out of that recognition and his own penitence of heart he gasped, "Lord, remember me when thou comest into thy kingdom" (Luke 23:42 KJV).

The cross of Christ changed the essential situation not only for the penitent thief but for every person who looks to Christ in the same faith. Jesus said that it would. After offering himself as the living bread and promising that whoever eats of this bread shall live, Jesus said, "The bread which I will give for the life of the world is my flesh" (v.51). Then he shocked the people listening to him by saying, "He who eats my flesh and drinks my blood has eternal life" (v.54) — figurative language that would not have seemed shocking if they had understood it as such. Every time we receive the Holy Communion we symbolically eat the flesh and drink the blood which Christ gave for the life of the world. We re-enact the death of Christ on the cross, the death that was for us, because it unites us with Christ's own life, a life that never ends.

Jesus Christ bridges the chasm between time and eternity. He is our "bridge to God" — a phrase which is the title of a book by the Rev Brian Hession, a Church of England clergyman, who wrote it in the period before his third chest operation. In 1954 his illness was diagnosed as terminal cancer, and he was given three days to live; but by his sheer determination to live longer and by his stubborn faith that God had a purpose for his life, he cheated this untimely death long enough to enable him to exercise an unusual ministry through his example and his writings. All over England there are people who are alive today only because his books gave them the will to live. I used to receive letters of serene courage and hope from a crippled girl who corresponded regularly with him. For seven years he lived on the edge of an abyss, seven years of incurable suffering and pain on borrowed time. He knew what he was talking about when he said that "this is a tough world," and he earned the right to describe the fruit of Christian faith as "a sense of spiritual guts." His book closes with these words.

> Jesus is such an extraordinary person, such a miraculous person, speaking with such authority, that I bow down before his Majesty and am prepared to believe what He said and trust my whole soul and being to Him. In so doing I have the confidence that I shall cross the bridge, which is Jesus Christ, to God in my final hour.[40]

Jesus Christ changed Brian Hession's essential situation. How else explain his incredible courage and remarkable Christian ministry in the face of suffering and death? Christ became the bridge not only over his pain but over his mortality. He could lose his health, his career, his family, lose his life on earth, yet still look forward with serenity and hope because he had found in Christ — not only in the promise of Christ but in Christ himself — the secret of a life that never ends. We also shall possess that secret if we believe the promise, "I am the living bread that came down from heaven; if anyone eats of this bread, he will live for ever."

III The third thing to notice is that we are asked not only to believe Christ's offer but to *accept it, trust it, and put it to the test*. We do *eat* bread. We don't just talk about its nutritive qualities or admire it through a bakeshop window. We have to feed on bread, digest and assimilate it until it becomes part of our own flesh and blood. By the same token, it's not enough to talk about Christ or even worship him. We have to feed on Christ — there is no other word to describe it. We have to absorb his teaching, his character, his ways and his spirit; we have to assimilate the virtue that is in him until his heart beats in our breast, his mind thinks in our brain, and his power has passed into us and becomes our power.

A single word describes what it means to feed on Christ, the word "commitment." The disciples knew what that meant. After Jesus made those immense claims, recorded in the sixth chapter of John's gospel, many of his former followers deserted him, giving the reason, "This is a hard saying; who can listen to it?" (v. 60). Jesus then asked the twelve, "Will you also go away?" (v.69). Peter spoke for them all when he replied, "Lord, to whom shall we go? You have the words of eternal life" (v.68). That's what it means to be committed — turning to Christ when others turn away, turning to him in the total trust that, although some of his words are difficult to understand, they are the words of eternal life, the life that never ends.

Does that mean that we shall live forever as Jesus promised? At the very least it means that we shall live; and that is surely important, because that's where eternal life begins. What person wants to live forever if his life has not been worth living in the first place? The melancholy Hamlet hoped that he would not live after death, voicing his dilemma in the famous soliloquy, "To be or not to be: that is the question." As he saw it, life on earth had been so terrible that more of the same thing after death could only be more terrible. Contrast him with the apostle Paul in his final imprisonment who faced the very dilemma of not knowing whether to choose life or death, because each is so wonderful. Life is wonderful because it is Christ, death more wonderful because it is more of Christ. "For me to live is Christ," said Paul. Therefore he could add, "and to die is gain" (Phil. 1:21).

Yet Paul still had to die, as we all have to die. Surely that is still our essential situation in spite of the cross of Christ and in spite of our commitment to him. Yes indeed! It happened to Jesus himself. On Good Friday he died and was buried. Like old Jacob Marley he was as dead as a doornail. "But God raised him up," declared Peter, "having loosed the pangs of death, because it was not possible for him to be held by it" (Acts 2:24 RSV). Christ promises that we shall live forever, not because we are incapable of dying, but because we shall share his resurrection life. Three times in this chapter of John's gospel (vv.40,44,54) he gave the same promise concerning the person who is committed to him: "I will raise him up at the last day."

Even during his earthly ministry the historic Jesus raised the dead to life. One of them was Lazarus, the brother of Mary and Martha in Bethany (John 11:1vv). Eugene O'Neill wrote a play called *Lazarus Laughed*[41] which follows that character from Bethany to Greece. In a square at Athens he meets the half-crazed and cruel Gaius Caligula who has been chosen by the Emperor Tiberius as his successor. When spies inform Caligula that the people hate him, he retorts, "Let them hate — so long as they fear us! We must keep death dangling in before their eyes . . . . I like to watch men die." Suddenly this monster of a man is confronted by Lazarus who has the appearance of "a stranger from a far land." He accuses Lazarus of teaching people to laugh at death and threatens him with execution. Lazarus looks into his face, laughs softly "like a man in love with God" and answers, "Death is dead, Caligula. Death is dead."

That is the *new* essential situation created by Christ in his resurrection. He has destroyed death, and death is now dead. Therefore we can trust his gracious offer, "I am the living bread which came down from heaven; if anyone eats of this bread, he will live for ever." We can do more than trust it. We can accept it and stake our lives on it now and for all eternity. We can commit ourselves to Jesus Christ — the best and the greatest.

NOTES

1 By William Herbert Carruth, 1859–1924.
2 From *The Hound of Heaven*.
3 John A.T. Robinson, *Exploration Into God* (Stanford: Stanford University Press, 1967), p. 119.
4 Frederick B. Speakman, *Love is Something You Do* (Westwood, N.J.: Fleming H. Revell Company, 1959), p. 120.
5 New York: Avon Books, 1974.
6 Malcolm Muggeridge, *Jesus Rediscovered* (London: Collins Fontana Books, 1969), p. 98.
7 Jimmy Carter, *Why Not the Best?* (Nashville, Tennessee: The Broadman Press, 1975).
8 Deane William Ferm, "'The Road Ahead in Theology' Revisited," in *The Christian Century*, 9 May 1979, p. 527.
9 J.H. Oldham, *Life is Commitment* (London: Student Christian Movement Press, Ltd., 1953), p. 24.
10 Cited in Louis H. Evans, *Youth Seeks a Master* (New York: Fleming H. Revell Company, 1946), p. 88.
11 As told by Harold B. Walker in *Power to Manage Yourself* (New York: Harper and Brothers, 1955), pp. 19–20.
12 Lesslie Newbigin, *The Household of God* (London: S.C.M. Press, 1953), pp. 100–01.
13 New York, Evanston and London: Harper and Row, 1967, p. 84.
14 New York, Evanston and London: Harper and Row, 1975.
15 David E. Roberts, *The Grandeur and Misery of Man* (New York: Oxford University Press, 1855).
16 Told by Robert E. Luccock in *The Power of His Name* (New York: Harper and Brothers, 1960), p. 129.
17 Evans, *Youth Seeks a Master*, pp. 104–05.
18 Charles W. Colson, *Born Again* (Toronto, New York, London: Bantam Books, 1976), p. 144.
19 Told by W.E. Sangster in *The Craft of Sermon Illustration* (Philadelphia: The Westminster Press, 1950), p. 39.
20 Bertrand Russell, *Why I Am Not A Christian* (London: George Allen & Unwin Ltd., 1957), p. 11.
21 Paul Scherer, *We Have This Treasure* (New York and London: Harper and Brothers, 1944), p. 90.
22 New York, and Evanston: Harper and Row, 1962, p. 114ff.
23 Michael Bordeaux, *Opium of the People* (London: Faber and Faber, 1965), pp. 148–50.

24 Translated from the Sermon of the Rev J. Scheffler by the Rev John Wesley.
25 London: Collins Fontana, 1965, p. 104.
26 Eberhard Busch, *Karl Barth*, tr. John Bowden (Philadelphia: Fortress Press, 1976), p. 340.
27 New York: The Viking Press, copyright 1947.
28 New York: Simon and Shuster, 1973.
29 Helmut Thielicke, *Our Heavenly Father* (New York: Harper and Row, 1960), pp. 55-56.
30 New York: Warner Books, 1974, p. 111.
31 London: Collins Fountain Books, 1977, p. 146.
32 New York: Bantam Books (Random House), 1971.
33 D.R. Davies, *In Search of Myself* (London: Geoffrey Bles, 1961), p. 175.
34 Alvin Toffler, *Future Shock*, p. 251ff.
35 New York: Viking Press.
36 John Howard Griffin, *Black Like Me* (New York: The New American Library/ Signet Books, 1960), pp. 15-16.
37 New York: Association Press, 1968, p. 66.
38 *Guideposts*, March 1959.
39 *The Christian Century*, 12 July 1967.
40 Brian Hession, *Bridge to God* (London: Peter Davies, 1961), p. 196.
41 New York: Random House.